Life Review in H
Social Care

The key to gaining awareness of the present and preparing for the future lies in our understanding of the past, yet there is little coverage of this topic in the existing psychology and counselling literature. How can people improve themselves by greater self-knowledge?

Jeff and Christina Garland break new ground in making a straightforward presentation of the theory and practice of the everyday process of life review, which is a therapeutic approach for helping clients make sense of their past, and can be used to help change undesirable behaviour and plan for the future. The theory and structure of the life review process is examined, and clinical examples of how it works in practice are given; this includes interviews both with 'narrators' (people engaged in life review) and 'listeners' (health and social care professionals). These examples demonstrate how professionals can use life review to help their clients overcome difficulties in their lives and face the future with confidence.

Life Review will appeal to trainees and practitioners in occupational, developmental, clinical, and health psychology, social work, counselling, psychotherapy, and nursing.

Jeff Garland is an Honorary Consultant with Oxfordshire Mental Healthcare Trust. He has been a clinical psychologist since 1967. **Christina Garland** trained as a psychiatric nurse before emigrating to Australia, where she is now an Information Officer with the Council on the Ageing in Sydney.

Life Review in Health and Social Care

A Practitioner's Guide

Jeff and Christina Garland

First published 2001
by Brunner-Routledge
27 Church Road, Hove, East Sussex BN3 2FA

Simultaneously published in the USA and Canada
by Taylor & Francis Inc
325 Chestnut Street, Philadelphia PA 19106

Brunner-Routledge is an imprint of the Taylor & Francis Group

Typeset in Times by Graphicraft Ltd, Hong Kong
Printed and bound in Great Britain by TJ International Ltd,
Padstow, Cornwall
Cover design by Terry Foley

British Library Cataloguing in Publication Data
A catalogue record for this book is available from the British Library

Library of Congress Cataloging in Publication Data
Garland, Jeff, 1938–
Life review : the process of knowing yourself / Jeff and Christina Garland.
p. cm.
Includes bibliographical references and indexes.
ISBN 0-415-21655-9 — ISBN 0-415-21656-7 (pbk.)
1. Autobiographical memory. 2. Reminiscing. 3. Self-perception. 4. Self-evaluation. I. Garland, Christina, 1968–
II. Title.
BF378.A87 G37 2001
153.1′3—dc21

00-069670

ISBN 0-415-21655-9 (hbk)
ISBN 0-415-21656-7 (pbk)

Actually we have it all wrong, when we say look forward to the future. The future is a void and we walk, so as to say, blindly with our backs towards it. At best we see what we have left behind.

(Fritz Perls, 1969)

Contents

Preface

Sitting as a student at the feet of Professor Leslie Hearnshaw at the University of Liverpool in the 1960s, the senior author heard him open the module 'Introduction to Psychology' with a guiding principle. In the East, the professor intoned, there was a tradition of inspired passivity. In the West, by contrast, a culture of uninspired activity prevailed. 'Here', he announced, 'let us aim to have the best of both worlds.'

With this text, we are still hopeful after all these years, in striving for the best of both worlds in the integration of theory and practice relating to adult life review. We examine the status of life review within the developmental process; and show how human services may draw on life review in working with clients.

Our experience in working with students, teachers, researchers, and practitioners has uncovered a strongly felt need for such integration; and frequently we have been asked for a book that gathers the many strands of thinking and practice, and 'brings it all together'.

Life review is used in at least eight areas of activity: counselling; psychotherapy, individual and group; family therapy; career planning; reminiscence in everyday life; autobiography and biography; oral history; and the study of life span development. We shall be giving particular attention to the first two of these.

There are many gaps and overlaps in a scattered literature. We have pieced together a map, finding that in spite of disparities among previous explorers the sum of their charts adds up.

We ask you not to mistake the map for the territory: learning by doing is vital; and we encourage you to appreciate that knowing yourself is a prerequisite for knowing others.

Introduction

For brevity's sake, life review will usually be called 'review'. The individual whose life experience is the subject of review will be called 'the narrator'. The target of the narration, usually one or more others, is called 'the listener' (such listening is likely to be active, with engagement in dialogue, including seeking clearer expression, prompting, probing, and challenging). As review can be carried out independently, without an external listener, 'listener' is occasionally used to denote a narrator self-monitoring.

Three modes of review are introduced in Chapter 1, and discussed in Chapters 4 and 6. The first, and most widely used, is everyday relatively unstructured and non-specific reflection. This activity may be channelled into two other forms: organised activity in an individual or group approach in which semi-structured questioning is undertaken on selected topics; and review in a setting of counselling or therapy, individual or group, in a more intensive process, with a therapeutic alliance imposing structure, and an agenda of identifying specific issues for change.

Review is presented in Chapter 1 as to be understood most usefully in the context of life span development, and the concepts of mapping, metaphor, tasks, themes, and transitions are commended as particularly appropriate. While recognising its significance for older adults, review is seen as relevant across the life span. The modes are located in the context of life span development theory, particularly in relation to thinking on mapping, metaphors, tasks, themes, and transitions; and autobiographical memory. Drawing in methods and techniques that use review, although they are not labelled as such, widens the perspective.

In Chapter 2, narrators' reasons for choosing to review are appraised in terms of: curiosity; self-presentation; taking stock; assessment; and support.

The structure of review is described in Chapter 3 as including: recognition of readiness; exploring and interpreting life events; shaping time; and planning for the future. The involvement of review is outlined in: everyday reminiscence; autobiography and biography; oral history; life span development; career planning; counselling; family therapy; and individual psychotherapy. Its status in practice and ethical framework is considered.

Seven interrelated elements that appear to be of particular importance in determining whether or not review is effective in enhancing the psychological well-being of the narrator are identified in Chapter 4 as 'active ingredients'. These are: positive reinforcement built into the process; accepting experiences and conclusions that the narrator wishes to continue to own and be responsible for; letting go of experiences and conclusions that the narrator sees as harmful or no longer relevant; taking control; insight; reframing; and commitment to change. Development of a model of how these interact within the modes of life review is discussed.

Procedures and skills for engaging in each of the modes are presented in an interactive style that encourages the reader to learn through taking part. Over the first seven chapters a total of twenty scenarios set out choice points and pose questions to elicit preferred options for engaging in life review. Chapter 9 takes up the scenarios in turn and examines options and outcomes.

Ten of the scenarios are to be found in Chapter 5, 'Narrators and their stories', and this chapter opens up the subject of practitioner skills. Readers who want to 'get down to business' may choose to start with Chapter 5 and continue with 6 and 7 on skills and their use. Thinking points are used throughout the text to draw out opinions. In Chapters 6 and 7 exercises in conducting a personal life review invite involvement.

Issues relating to the evaluation of life review and its development are confronted, and scope for extending qualitative investigation is examined, in Chapter 8. We acknowledge that thorough appraisal of the outcomes of life review needs more intensive study and look at prospects for establishing evidence-based practice.

A postscript gives key references, audio-visual aids and other learning resources that we would commend to readers; and an appendix includes questions that may be used by a listener.

Chapter 1

Review in context

SUMMARY From childhood on, life review is an everyday activity. As a resource in personal development, counselling, and therapy, it can take many forms, be engaged in by individuals or groups, and have a variety of functions and outcomes. It draws on autobiographical memory and focused reminiscence to maintain or modify coping strategies. A framework for understanding review is life span developmental theory, particularly the concepts of mapping, metaphor, tasks, themes, and transition.

Review helps people to learn to know themselves and others, and to be more fully human: it is a vital resource. But it is not a panacea. While it can enable a person or group to make a balanced appraisal of progress and to evolve psychologically in order to get to grips with a challenging world, misused (for example, by a narrator who selectively recalls unhappy events), it can entrench resistance to change, and deepen misery. Also, as Phillips (1999) warns, it is part of our own life story to try to keep control of the stories people tell about us. For every narrator there is always the story of stories I don't want people, including myself, to tell about myself. The listener should respect due reticence.

Defining review

Throughout this text review is understood as being a continuing reflexive process starting in childhood with the development of autobiographical memory. It can have three stages: focusing on what has been learned about self in relation to others; considering whether this learning is still relevant; and recognising what should be retained, revising what is unclear, and discarding what is no longer required.

It is a distinctive way of using evaluative reminiscence (Molinari and Reichlin, 1984–5). As Ruth and Kenyon (1995) indicate, individuals are co-authors of their own stories, in that we shape the world and ourselves, and our world and other persons shape us. Edinberg (1985) sees review as having a multifaceted role: to aid the narrator in achieving new insight and peace of mind; to bring closure to troubling events through viewing them from a different perspective; and to restore as far as possible neglected skills or abilities.

The stages are not necessarily present in sequence in every episode of review. If it is being carried out without a listener, the narrator can be reluctant to look too closely at learning and need for change. If there is no listener then the narrator determines the meanings of 'relevant', 'unclear', and 'no longer necessary'. If there is a listener, this is usually negotiated between narrator and listener.

Review occurs in three modes. In the course of life, most of us engage in Mode 1 from time to time, in a relatively unstructured and non-specific way. On occasion – for example, when facing a transition or a crisis – this may become much more focused and intensive; and the narrator may seek out one or more listeners for support. In Mode 2, the reviewer takes up his or her story as a planned activity, sometimes in a group, with a semi-structured approach, going through selected topics with one or more committed listeners. Mode 3 offers a relatively structured and specific opportunity to the narrator or narrators experiencing problems in everyday living, to work with one or more counsellors or therapists, and consider changes in the way a story is viewed and lived. These modes may overlap to some extent, and it is not suggested that any one of these is necessarily superior to the others. They are discussed in more detail in Chapters 4 and 6.

Narrative psychology (McLeod, 1997, Crossley, 2000, and Payne, 2000) sets accounts of human behaviour in a storytelling framework. Review often proceeds by fits and starts, using contemplation, soliloquy, and monologue, as well as dialogue, with an episodic and intermittent course rather than a continuous progression. Narrative psychology puts forward a post-modern perspective, contending that what is knowable essentially is immediate awareness of living expressed in the stories we tell others and ourselves.

Varieties of review

As Hillman (1999) points out, a life has a huge inventory. The individual may be likened to a warehouse keeper running a LIFO system

– last in, first out – clearing new input in order to preserve space for stock that has been there for a long time. With progress towards maturity and character formation, the warehouse keeper may be expected to spend more time in the back of the premises recovering and refurbishing the past, as character seeks to understand itself.

Review can occur in a momentary fashion, with one or more brief episodes, at exceptional times of unexpected upheaval or with the occurrence of epiphanies (moments of enlightenment). An individual who makes a practice of mulling over daily experience can conduct review in a sustained way as a form of meditation. For some people the process may be protracted, running in the background over an extended period. As DeSalvo (1999) illustrates, there is an extensive literature of autobiographical 'healing' of psychological trauma. For others, review may be largely absent, or engaged in only sporadically, with self-questioning (for example, 'where did I go wrong?') only under immediate pressure of outside events.

It may be private or public; be conducted by an individual, or carried out by a couple, family, or other system (see Byng-Hall, 1995, for analysis of family scripts); and it may be structured within the remit of counselling, individual or family therapy, or some other form of professional intervention. However, as McLeod (1997) suggests, it may be open to doubt that psychotherapy, with an individualistic, specialist and morally neutral stance, is positioned to enable people to tell stories that need to be presented in social, cultural, and moral context.

White and Epson (1990) note that human nature and 'self' is socially constructed from moment to moment, with knowledge and practices of culture informing our life and thought. A central consideration in their work is that persons generally ascribe meaning to their lives by plotting their experience into stories that shape lives and relationships.

As a therapeutic approach, review has distinctive features that call to mind cognitive behavioural therapy. It keeps returning to the present to find how 'then' has shaped 'now'; it questions whether decisions taken in the past should continue to influence present or future; and if the answer is 'no' it identifies how such decisions can be challenged or replaced (Garland and Kemp, 1996). From an objective standpoint the main aim could be described as being to increase insight and psychological well-being based on a secure sense of self-identity in relation to others.

Review does not necessarily have a beginning, middle, or an end. Frequently it may be postponed or sidetracked. When existence is marginal, so that survival from day to day is doubtful, it may be abandoned completely. Even when it is used consistently, it may be biased by the distortions of an individual's negative expectations and by the pressures of social prejudice, so that it becomes counter-productive.

Review in action

We are in accord with psychologists who give particular emphasis to the consideration that the brain creates meaning and that a human being can be most usefully understood in terms of the way meaning is processed and understood. We propose that the most productive way of viewing individual differences in human personality is through examining the variety of ways in which persons shape and interpret the meaning of their experience (Rowe, 1995).

People normally use autobiographical memory, reminiscence, and review throughout conscious and reflective life. It is not always easy to distinguish between these, because in practice they are interrelated. However, not all autobiographical memory or reminiscence can be construed automatically as review, and our first scenario may help the distinction become clear.

In the following scenario, the statement by Alice in the last paragraph and the thoughts that led up to it we would see as potential steps in review, or at least an opening gambit. A generalisation drawn from experience is made about how a life has been lived; and there is implicit understanding of potential for learning that may be applied to present and future behaviour. It is of course possible that 'Alice' will not be interested in applying the learning she hints at. She may consider that 'feeling bad' is an interesting, potentially dramatic, state that she would not want to quit; or even have come to the decision that it is no more than she deserves. Or, more prosaically, dealing with the topic may be derailed by one of the many distractions that can affect a private discussion in a public place.

Scenario 1

From the next table in a café you can hear Alice talking to her friend Tilda, about their relationships with men (she refers to them as 'chaps'). You do not wish to eavesdrop but Alice and Tilda talk loudly, as is the way with Oxford undergraduates, and you cannot avoid hearing them.

Alice begins by drawing on autobiographical memory to describe incidents from the social life of the past week of their term. Her confidante, who has shared some of these experiences, contributes some corrections and other amendments from her own memory. Alice appears to accept some of these and lets others pass without comment.

Tilda begins to reminisce about her earlier experiences with males in her school life, but Alice is not interested, dismissing that as 'kids' stuff'. However, she begins to look thoughtful, and is silent for a few moments. Alice then announces, as though she has realised something for the first time: 'You know, my problem is I always end up going out with chaps who are less (how can I put it?) mature than me. And I end up feeling bad.' She is speaking in earnest, and when she has finished each is silent.

- **If you were Alice and wanted to engage in review, how would you continue the dialogue?**
- **If you were Tilda and wanted to listen to Alice constructively, how would you respond?**
- **Taking the roles of Alice and Tilda alternately, how would you continue to explore the implications of what Alice has said?**
- **Consider from your own life, or that of someone you know, an example of a 'my problem is . . .' situation. How could this be resolved in life review?**

(See Chapter 9, p. 143, for authors' comments.)

Not just for older people

This text gives full attention to the use of review by older adults, which is indeed a widely used application worthy of interest in its own right. It is not to be confined to the well-known definition of Butler (1963), who revived the concept of life review for older adults. He introduces this as: 'A naturally occurring, universal mental process characterised by the progressive return to consciousness of past experiences, and, particularly, the resurgence of unresolved conflicts: simultaneously and normally, these revived experiences can be surveyed and reintegrated' (p. 66).

He sees this as prompted by the realisation of approaching dissolution and death, and the inability to maintain one's sense of personal invulnerability. This can result in reorganisation, including achievement of wisdom, serenity, and increased self-assurance. Butler's seminal paper was the precursor to rapid growth in review therapy, concerned with helping clients restructure their past into a positive and integrated story (Lewis and Butler, 1974). In directing the attention of researchers and clinicians, the concept of review as a therapy came to be focused mainly on middle life and old age.

Many other writers developed this theme, including Verwoerdt (1981), for whom the task of review is to integrate life lived with the one that might have been. He sees this as a constructive and active process, which could achieve a sense of 'closure' and harmony. Recognising that it could be far-ranging in mood, from nostalgic recall to marked unhappiness, leisurely or urgent, he views it as a vehicle for communicating a set of social and cultural values to a younger generation.

Discussing reminiscence in relation to the therapy needs of older adults, Garland (1994) suggests that life review therapy for them could be summed up as

> a process of systematic reflection in later life, involving a therapist and a client or clients, and focusing on understanding life history and its implications for current coping strategies. A positive outcome would be assessed in terms of resolution of conflicts, and improved well-being based on a sense of self-acceptance and having come to terms with life.
>
> (p. 21)

Review is not confined to tying up loose ends, and putting one's psychological house in order. In a continuing process, with many ups and downs, it is not uncommon for narrators to remain at odds with life and to choose to leave conflicts unresolved, yet feel positive about the process because, after due reflection, they have reaffirmed their decision not to be reconciled.

A family saga

In this chapter, review will in effect tell its own story and introduce itself. This narrative of its growth can be viewed as a condensed family saga, in the sense that it is most usefully considered in a context of relationships with life span development, autobiographical memory, and reminiscence.

As Bromley (1990) explains, these are all closely connected with adults' ability to maintain and develop a sense of self, based on historical continuity. Both individuality and social identity are based on being able to recall psychologically significant events and being able to recognise who other people are.

Life span development

The life span perspective views human development as occurring across the life span (Sugarman, 1986), with most theorists proposing a series of critical stages. Transitional phases and significant life events, it is suggested, punctuate these. An individual can only be understood in the context of a personal history ('read like a book'). Baltes *et al.* (1980) view life span perspective as a family of theoretical propositions:

1. Development is a long-term process – throughout life there is potential for both continuous growth (gradual, incremental, cumulative, and quantitative), and discontinuous development (rapid, innovative, substantial, and qualitative).
2. It is multidimensional and multidirectional. Different elements – career, family, intellectual, social – may take relatively distinct developmental directions. Conflicts can be expected between role of child and role of parent, role of employee and role of home-maker. Even within one of these roles, there are several different criteria for measuring progress.
3. It involves loss as well as gain. Growth and decline sometimes come together. To make a decision to move on in life is to sacrifice possibilities, and lose something of the past, while opening up new opportunities and relationships. Personal growth brings risk, as Gould (1980) understands, pointing out that, as we push at psychological boundaries to gain a sense of inner freedom, we simultaneously undermine the illusion that we can do this and remain safe from major risks.
4. Plasticity is normal. There is potential for substantial variability in the way each individual copes with development at any point in time. While steps in developmental progress during the first few months or years of life are likely to follow a relatively fixed time-table, in later life a much wider range of possibilities tends to open up.
5. The historically and culturally embedded nature of development should be appreciated. Cultural differences are important, and it is inappropriate to transfer from one social group to another ideas about development. Historical differences mean that the past is an uncertain and unreliable guide to the future.

6 Development is the outcome of transactions between each person and that person's environment. The human being is an active organism as part of an active environment, in a two-way interchange.
7 Life span development is a multidisciplinary concept. Input from anthropology, sociology, psychology, biology, chemistry, and other sciences is needed for its full understanding. Psychology is applied to describing processes within the individual, interactions between individuals and their personal settings, and interactions between different settings. In effect, aspects of the developmental process are usually most usefully considered from a both/and, rather than an either/or viewpoint.

You work for an agency that advises couples on relationship issues, and you have been asked to counsel Laura and Adam who are in their mid-thirties. Each has been married before. After six months their marriage is in trouble. They quarrel frequently and Laura wants a separation.

Adam has initiated their referral. He is critical of Laura's continuing to 'encourage' men she knew before their marriage by behaving with them on social occasions 'as if nothing had happened'. He claims that this must mean she has a problem of 'being promiscuous in her head', which as a counsellor you must know how to deal with. Laura feels that Adam has a problem – 'long-standing insecurity' stemming from his disturbed childhood during which several relationships within his family of origin ended abruptly. He attacks her verbally and physically and he appears abnormally jealous of what she sees as being simply everyday friendships.

- **Thinking point**
  Examine the propositions of Baltes *et al.* With these in mind formulate questions that you would wish to ask to help you understand this couple.

Rapid growth

Life span development has grown rapidly as an area of study, particularly over the last twenty years, for a number of reasons. The topic is intrinsically interesting, as it deals with the complexities of developing as a changing individual in a changing society; it helps in the understanding of what is meant by psychological well-being or normality; and it gives scope for judging the significance of instances of deviation from age-appropriate behaviour.

This area of study has been a relatively late developer, and we suggest that this is not surprising. There has been a body of psychodynamic opinion that adults don't develop significantly; adult life has not been seen as susceptible to developmental analysis; adults tend to be less accessible to researchers between the hours of nine and five; it is difficult to get funding, because expensive social problems are seen as clustering in early or late life; and adult researchers may be uncomfortable studying peers, as this is too close to home.

Objections

A number of objections to life span theorising have been raised. Until the 1970s, most psychologists believed that qualitative advances in development did not occur after adolescence (Alexander and Langer, 1990). Cognitive, affective, moral, self, and consciousness development in adults was given little attention by researchers. Although this position has changed, some scientists and clinicians still feel uncomfortable with life span development as a subject of serious study. They point out that it tends to be all-embracing, taking in 'life, the universe, and everything'; and that its concepts are not always well-defined.

Considering theories of successful ageing, Ryff (1989) points to: lack of theory guiding research; narrow conceptions of well-being (seen as the absence of significant abnormality, rather than in positive terms); neglect of possibility for continued growth and development; and failure to take sufficient account of concepts of positive ageing as being human constructions liable to cultural variations and historical change. Bromley (1988) sees adult ageing as a disorderly process of biological and behavioural disorganisation, and as fundamentally unsuitable for developmental understanding since it lacks the coherence of development in early life.

Other critics have argued that many of the early influential studies were difficult to generalise from because they had a preponderance of white middle-class American males; and that for the disadvantaged, struggling to survive, preoccupation with personal development would not be an issue. Also, on many life span issues it is difficult to gather reliable data. For example, growing loneliness in later life may be covered up because: it is socially undesirable to admit loneliness; it is too painful to discuss; many respondents practise stoicism; there is a tendency to accept 'the devil you know'; scepticism or fear relating to possible outcome of admitting loneliness. Technical problems for quantitative analysis abound; and life span evidence is a messy mixture (autobiographical accounts, semi-structured interviews, relatively small samples, and few long-term studies).

As in almost any area of scientific study, investigators are divided among themselves. For example, Riegel (1976) swims against the mainstream as a critic of stage theories, which he dismisses as an enormous waste of time and effort, an exercise in futility. He views development as 'ceaseless flux', within which at least four dimensions (inner-biological, individual-psychological, cultural-sociological, and outer-physical) are constantly interacting to create problems, raise questions, and bring changes for individuals and systems. Schroots (1995) invokes chaos theory, noting that in the open system of a life a single fluctuation may become so powerful that it shatters the form of a narrative, so that it is inherently impossible to determine whether the story will disintegrate or suddenly shift into a new form.

As Blackmore (1999) notes, if one concentrates on the present moment, paying attention to everything equally and letting go of thoughts that may come up, the idea of a 'self' who is experiencing these events tends to fall away. In her provocative view of the human being as a 'meme machine' or processor of units of cultural transmission, imitation, beliefs, ideas, and ways of thinking, the notion of an emerging 'I', a 'me' in charge, which has been a focal point within the study of individual development, may be nothing more than a temporary conglomeration of genes, phenotypes, memes and memeplexes.

Most theorists unthinkingly enshrine the self as an executive agent endowed with free will and striving to maximise gain and minimise pain, without pausing to consider the philosophical assumptions on which this view of humanity is based. It is possible to contend, as Blackmore does, that the 'self' as a distinct and unitary entity is a misleading fiction, and that in social behaviour the individual may have recourse to a psychological wardrobe of 'selves' to present in different situations.

Advantages

Although many complexities and contradictions remain in the growing literature on life span development, it does offer a number of advantages for the understanding and application of review. This is unsurprising in view of the presentation by Baltes *et al.* of life span development thinking as being concerned with description, explanation, and optimisation of development in the life course from conception to death.

For Sugarman (1996), counselling is grounded in life span developmental psychology, as development centres on notions of improvement, movement in the direction of perfection, with increasing control over one's life, being self-reliant, fulfilling personal potential, and accepting responsibility for one's actions. As she points out, the goal of self-empowerment, which is an objective of life span development, is in accord with the overall aim of counselling: 'to provide an opportunity for the client to work towards living in a more satisfying and resourceful way'.

Biographies

Life span development theorists and those engaging in review have a mutual interest in the use of biographical material. Biographies can be seen as attempted solutions to the challenge facing each individual of attempting to make sense of an existence which can seem chaotic in its randomness. In a sense they are passports that purport to create a consistent identity across the life span in the face of characteristic ambiguities and crises encountered in the course of being alive. Biographical narrative can be understood as an instrument for framing a system of rules whereby an individual squeezes quarts of experience into a pint pot container labelled 'meaning'.

With increasing affluence, the more economically and culturally privileged classes are able to elaborate their ideas about what constitutes a satisfactory social network and a lifestyle that is expansive and varied, and seek to develop their narratives. Older people, too, can and increasingly will avail themselves of vehicles for biographical work, including counselling and psychotherapy. Universities of the Third Age, research institutes, specialised counselling services, pressure groups, and specialist Internet facilities are among the many resources at their disposal.

It is necessary to construct continuity in an ongoing way – processing past, present, and future as biography to amalgamate a complex world. Many aspects of everyday life, such as the design and decoration of home surroundings (Rubinstein, 1995), become ways of projecting a biography. This ability can be trained and exercised in a culture where focus groups, documentary-soaps, radio phone-ins, and talk radio can all play a part in democratising communication.

A changing world

The shifting nature of grandparenthood is an example of a changing world. There is interplay of greater occupational mobility, grandparents with a life of their own, and new patterns in divorce and remarriage. There is disengagement, with more children leaving home when young, who may or may not have regular contact with their parents, and who may be unwilling to resume a close relationship much later in life. A modern grandparent is more likely to be expected to retain personal responsibility for his or her own life course, its decisions and choices. There will be no point in time when a fit older person can give over such responsibility to someone else and lean back to rest. In these circumstances the stories that grandparents as culture carriers have shared with grandchildren become a diminishing resource in limited demand.

At the same time, a person retains core identity and a sense of continuity, experiencing change as gradual and incremental. The concept of narrative construction is capable of encompassing how individuals maintain a sense of coherence – a sense of being the same person they always have been – despite the gradual incremental changes associated with ageing, and despite major life disruptions.

Starr (1983) offers a social phenomenological theory of the life course. This accounts for how people generate and make meaning of the changes and stages in their lives, and in turn how they relate to those happenings which can seem to be of an arbitrary nature, with a life of their own. 'Biographical work' – the process individuals go through to search for integrative accounts to provide overall intelligibility for their lives – is at the centre of Starr's thinking.

Search for meaning

Kaufman (1986) uses individuals' life stories to understand the interrelationships between old age, personal reflection, and identity. In his view, people 'account' for their life through their stories. They make them logical and coherent with a sense of naturalness and rightness. They select, define, classify, and organise experience to present a life and its meaning.

Hillman (1999) cautions that seeking for meaning can come too soon, contending that the purpose of life is to live it, and knowing comes later. He recommends that memoirs, autobiography, and deep investigations of long-term psychotherapy probably should not be engaged in before 60. Review, he advises, needs the modesty of an apprentice embarking on an adventure. Taken up prematurely, it produces inflated subjectivity, not character, and releases just one more inflated 'me' entering a world already crowded with expanded egos.

There are five aspects of life span developmental thinking that we present as appearing to be of special relevance in this search for meaning: mapping; metaphors; tasks; themes; and transitions.

Mapping

For all concerned with reviewing a life, it can be helpful to have one or more points of reference to confirm where a narrator stands in relation to others of a similar age and background.

An individual's development may be charted by life crises (Erikson, 1980). Research in anthropology and education, and biographical study of such contrasting individuals as Gandhi and Hitler, has underlined the significance of critical steps, crucial periods of heightened vulnerability and increased potential. Erikson linked these with moments of decision between regression and progress through stages of psychosocial development. The classic 'mid-life crisis' may have been a self-fulfilling prophecy, and it has been suggested (Sheehy, 1996) that the concept of middle age might usefully be abolished, to be replaced by the notion of a 'second adulthood' beginning at 45.

An alternative viewpoint is that stages reflect impact of age-related social roles and expectation rather than influence of an individual's maturation. This is developed by Neugarten (1977), who concentrates on the influence of external occurrences and markers, an age-graded system and a prescriptive timetable for the ordering of life events. People are aware of a 'social clock' (Schlossberg *et al.*, 1977), which enables them to estimate whether they are 'on time', 'early', or 'late' for significant life events; blatant deviations make them feel uncomfortable and this can be picked up by others.

Metaphors

Metaphors are invoked frequently by narrators struggling to convey meaning. In working with such stories it can be useful to explore links with structures of metaphor already established. A story makes sense of people's experiences, ordering them temporally according to a theme. Narrative is an extended metaphor within the process of compiling a story that is described as emplotment by Ricoeur (1984):

a story is integrated by putting together a chain of events so that they make sense in relation to each other.

Levinson *et al.* (1978), viewing the life cycle as four eras running from childhood and adolescence through to late adulthood, predictably liken these phases to the four seasons. Super (1980) lists the principal theatres for role playing as home, community, school, and workplace, but notes many other venues, including places of worship, unions, clubs and related social settings, and retirement homes. Across a range of settings nine major roles may be enacted (child, student, consumer of leisure, citizen, worker, spouse or partner, homemaker, parent, and retiree), with many other possibilities, such as sibling, worshipper, lover, reformer, and deviant options such as criminal.

Ford and Lerner (1992) liken the life course to:

> a continuous and somewhat unpredictable journey throughout life, sailing from seas that have become familiar into oceans as yet uncharted toward destinations to be imagined, defined, and redefined as the voyage proceeds, with occasional, often unpredictable, transformations of one's vessel and sailing skills and the oceans upon which one sails resulting from unforeseen circumstances.
>
> (p. 47)

Erikson uses the language of growth, taking from embryology the epigenetic principle that 'anything that grows has a ground plan, and out of this ground plan the parts arise, each part having its time of special ascendancy, until all forms have arisen to form a functioning whole' (1980, p. 53). Jung (1939) depicts the life course with a metaphor of the sun from sunrise through zenith to sunset. Each phase of the life course is viewed as having its own characteristics, potentialities, and limitations.

Tasks

Unfinished business can become a major concern of narrators, and the literature has identified a number of task agendas. Tasks are seen as being influenced by: maturational processes; social and environmental forces; and individual creativity. For example, choice of occupation depends on structure of labour market, local opportunities, and education, as well as individual aptitudes and ambition. Tasks can be difficult to pin down, yet intensely absorbing. Levinson *et al.* cite

Stage	Crisis
1. Birth to one year	Trust vs. mistrust
2. One to two years	Autonomy vs. shame and doubt
3. Three to five years	Initiative vs. guilt
4. Six to eleven years	Industry vs. inferiority
5. Adolescence	Identity vs. role confusion
6. Early adulthood	Intimacy vs. isolation
7. Middle age	Generativity vs. stagnation
8. Old age	Ego integrity vs. despair

Figure 1 Erikson's psychosocial stages

chasing 'The Dream' as having: 'The quality of a vision, an imagined possibility that generates excitement and vitality' (1978, p. 91).

Erikson (1963) presents eight stages of psychosocial development, each characterised by a developmental task expressed as an emotional crisis that needs to be resolved, in order to establish coping strength for cumulative ego development. Stages 5 to 8 would appear to be of particular relevance to life review.

The concept of ego integrity is of particular importance in thinking about review. Erikson defines it as:

> The acceptance of one's own and only life cycle and of the people who have become significant to it as something that had to be and that, by necessity, permitted of no substitutions. It thus means a new different love of one's parents, free of the wish that they should have been different, and an acceptance of the fact that one's life is one's own responsibility. It is a sense of comradeship with men and women of different times and of different pursuits, who have created orders and objects and sayings conveying human dignity and love.
>
> (1963, p. 104)

Erikson has been influential but his ideas can be challenged. For example, Peck (1968) suggested that the old-age stage needed to be broken down into at least three factors: ego differentiation vs. work role preoccupation ('am I valuable as a human being or only valuable because I can work?'); body transcendence vs. body preoccupation ('can I accept my ageing body for what it is and enjoy it?'); and ego transcendence vs. ego preoccupation. Commentators on stage theories have generally agreed that an end stage of final integrity or maturity expresses an ideal, not an attainable reality, and that the good life is a direction, not a destination (Rogers, 1967).

Themes

Themes emerge – they are the means by which people interpret and evaluate their life experiences and attempt to integrate these experiences to form a self-concept. Themes are organisational and explanatory markers that emerge as individuals relate their life stories. Although jobs, social activities, friendship patterns, family relations, living arrangements, and health status may change over the years, individuals, through the expression of themes, are able to connect and integrate the diverse experience of a lifetime. In this way, continuity is created and maintained symbolically in the individual life. Themes, as reformulated experience, can be considered building blocks of identity. Identity is founded on the significance of past experience, and the current rendering of meaningful symbols and events.

Many life stories are characterised by an overriding theme – sometimes by several interlocking ones – and relating them back to life span development thinking can illuminate such narratives. For Elsbree (1982), themes can be understood as generic plots for a life story. They include: establishing a home; engaging in a contest – battling with demands of conscience, or of parents; making a journey; enduring suffering – coming to terms with limitations and mistakes; and pursuing consummation.

Gould (1978) views adult development as being marked by preoccupations tending to be characteristic of a particular age frame. He sees these as having as a common feature movement towards accepting ourselves as the creators of our own lives, and away from being governed by ideas about what parents and authority figures wanted for us.

Transitions

Narrators frequently open or re-open reviews because they are at a point of transition and this should not be viewed in isolation. The complexity of the world can be overwhelming, as it changes so rapidly. People are often baffled by the unprecedented surprises that await them, and, unsure of who they are or why, they wind up struggling with the meaning of the fundamentals of life, with matters of birth, and development and death. At the same time, they are also borne up by tradition and, provided with inexhaustible resources for preserving and deepening their individual selves, are supported by their shared culture even in the midst of the most terrifying situations (Allan, 1994).

In occupational terms, Super (1980) describes the importance of decision points such as to enter or not enter the labour market, or settling on when, how, and where to retire. He notes how the individual can be assessed as approaching such transitions by: becoming aware of an impending career decision; formulating questions, and reviewing premises; identifying facts needed for an understanding of the situation; seeking data and evaluating it; identifying lines of action and weighing up outcomes and probabilities. He or she may then weigh alternatives in terms of values and objectives, select a plan of action, store the alternatives for future reference, and pursue the plan's opening steps while staying alert to the need for continuing review and modification along the way.

A framework for appreciating evolving life structure has been offered by Levinson *et al.* (1978). Structure is seen as the underlying pattern or design of a person's life at a given time, encompassing the characteristics of the person, and the person's relationships with people, things, institutions, places, and cultures. Existing on the boundary between person and environment, and a link between them, it evolves through transitional periods, alternating between structure-changing (exciting, frightening, upheaval) and structure-building (consolidation around key choices that have been made). Structures, these authors suggest, typically last from five to ten years, and then (no longer being able to accommodate changes in ourselves as the ways we relate to the world become outmoded) a new structure-changing phase comes in, itself lasting about five years.

In attempting to distinguish important changes in life course it is helpful to recognise three categories: universal age-graded changes; age-graded changes shared by a particular culture or sub-culture; and changes not associated with any particular age or life stage.

The San Francisco study by Lowenthal *et al.* (1975) indicates that in middle-aged couples most wives are not coping well, unsatisfied, seeing the future as empty and unpredictable, with increased likelihood of having considered suicide. Many are facing the 'empty nest' syndrome. Husbands are usually defensive, aware of lack of spontaneity or openness in the relationship. Both partners are increasingly concerned about health risks mounting in later life, and about the possibility of loss of security and enforced change in their lifestyle. Follow-up after mid-life transition indicates a shift in the direction of increased satisfaction only for those wives who had made major changes, such as drastically remodelling their home, or divorce, or a new career. For men, changes in family structure, threats to self-esteem from physical ageing, work pressures, and undue significance attached to relatively trivial sexual failure, could combine to produce problems that are sometimes labelled as mid-life crisis.

Autobiographical memory

Material for review is reached through remembering, and this process needs to be better understood. It is surprising that, with a few exceptions such as Kotre (1996), the literature on review tends to take little interest in the working of autobiographical memory.

Conway (1990) sees autobiographical memory as functioning to maintain the self, leading to emergence of a sense of the integrity of a personality. He considers the role of autobiographical memory in relation to review as being determined more by the existential challenges set by the past and the nature of current circumstances than by any predetermined cognitive process.

He cites the well-known account by Goethe that at the age of 4 he had thrown his parents' crockery out of a bedroom window to smash in the street below, and felt overpowering exhilaration as he did so. He connects this with the similar 'screen memories' reported by some of Freud's patients, and interpreted as screening memories of a desire to eject a sibling.

Memories lose specificity over time and become more generalised; older memories tend to be less vivid and less accessible; accuracy declines with time; and dating is imprecise. False memories can be deliberately implanted, and recognition tasks show a relatively high rate of false positive responses for false memories and false details of true memories. Experimental paradigms tend to exaggerate the fallibility of autobiographical memory and underestimate the amazing quantity and quality of information that is retained over a lifetime (Cohen, 1996).

Failure to recall early childhood memories in later life does not mean that young children cannot remember what happens to them. There is increasing evidence of striking memory ability in very young children, from field studies of the child's daily life. Nelson (1986) finds that, even before the age of 3, children show both knowledge of events in general and memories of specific events. Study of pre-sleep monologues in which each day's events were reviewed showed the emergence of knowledge structures based on recall of action sequences during the day and their outcomes.

Children's memory has been shown to be idiosyncratic. An adult cannot readily predict what a child will find memorable. Children remember what makes sense to them and fail to remember what does not make sense. Children's memory is also socially determined, since they tend to remember what they want to communicate. It is well known (Cohen, 1996) that normal adults may confabulate details of real memories. Can they produce completely false confabulated memories of events that never occurred at all?

Interest has been triggered by cases in which adults claim to have recovered repressed memories of sexual abuse that occurred in childhood. Recovery of these memories usually happens in the course of psychotherapy; and it has been suggested that the 'recovered events' never took place but have been implanted in vulnerable people by the therapeutic process (the False Memory Syndrome).

It is extremely difficult to find evidence one way or the other. Often supporting evidence that the abuse actually occurred as reported is absent; and existence of repressed memory is itself controversial. While it may be possible to recover memories late in life, it is not possible to be certain that all, or even most, of the events recounted as 'recovered' memories happened in the form in which they are reported.

The implication of this conclusion, for review, is that neither narrator nor listener should be unduly concerned with speculating about whether sensitive material raised in the review as remembered is necessarily based on fact. What is important is that it has been raised for discussion as affecting the present and future well-being of the narrator. Listener and narrator need to focus on what is presented rather than debate its origin.

Memory is a constructive process. Studies of eyewitnesses show that memory for accidents is shaped not merely by the original perception of events but also after the fact by incoming information and by the language used by questioners. Flashbulb memories – vivid recollections of the circumstances in which news of a historic event was heard – show apparent consistency because they become woven into a rehearsed narrative, rather than because original events were 'stamped in' to 'memory'.

Early memories in a life review have a similar quality. Kotre (1996) notes that what is called a 'first' memory means different things to different narrators. To some, the first memory is set in place as the childhood recollection with which they choose to open their story. For others, it is presented as the memory that is chronologically the earliest, the one that reaches furthest back in time. To still others, it is the childhood memory to which they give pride of place, the one to which they attach significance as a prototype or cause of other events.

Kotre decides that no matter which memory is designated as first, and no matter what meaning that label has, it and other early memories are not solely representations of the past. In many cases they are metaphors for narrators' unconscious intuitions about important life themes and about present conditions of their lives. In taking up early memories as often referring to founding events which took place 'in the beginning', Kotre is influenced by Adler (1957), who concludes that a person's earliest recollection could be understood as a subjective starting point, the beginning of autobiography. As the narrator's ongoing life changes, the content of these early memories changes too, as the following scenario shows.

Scenario 2

Joan, 79, is a resident in an old people's home, where Liz her principal carer found her 'a lovely lady but really difficult and demanding'. Joan had been an only child, and at first had offered as her first memory an idealised non-specific account of watching Christmas decorations being put up by her doting parents with a background of carols.

Over the months, as illness and physical infirmity progressed, her recollections darken, and spontaneously she relates her first 'real' memory. A toddler, she had been for a country stroll with her parents and was already tired when they came to a hill. Joan wanted to be carried but her parents refused and went up the hill anyway. They left her with fellow walkers, telling her to wait for them. Feeling small and lonely and terrified, she did so. She remembered this but had no memory of their coming back, 'although they must have done, mustn't they?'

This story becomes a starting point for Liz and Joan in developing an expanded narrative. Joan is supported in reflecting on what she had learned in her life experience, and in linking this to the present so that she can apply it in helping herself and those around her to cope with the challenge of her increasing dependency.

- **In Liz's place how might you set about helping Joan to develop this narrative?**
- **How would you proceed to link past and present?**
- **What goals would the two of you be working towards?**

(See Chapter 9, p. 144.)

Reminiscence

People of all ages reminisce: reminiscing is simply giving an account of what is remembered. The word has overtones of enjoyment, of being selective in dwelling on the past, and perhaps of seeing it through rose-coloured spectacles.

All kinds of memories may be the object of reminiscence – one example is the so-called 'hole in the road' phenomenon, whereby individuals engage in competitive reminiscence to describe deprivation in early life. (For example, one claims to have been brought up in 'a hovel', another counters with a declaration of having been raised in 'a pig-sty', while a third undermines both with a mournful, 'We lived in a hole in the road – if you can call it living.')

In a rural adult education class a group of over-sixties are exchanging memories of the deprivations of their early schooling. One recounts a 4-mile bus journey, minute by minute. Another relives a 6-mile walk, step by step. Others chime in, capping these experiences. Finally, someone on the edge of the group clears his throat and intervenes: 'School? Never heard the word 'til I was 10 years old, weeding turnips, and some passing townie said, "Why aren't you at school, young man?"'

'"School?" I said. "What's that?"'

Wong and Watt (1991) distinguish six types of reminiscence (which may overlap). Two that they propose as being associated with successful ageing are: integrative (acceptance of one's life, and resolution of past conflicts and negative life events); and instrumental (using recollection of, and drawing from, past plans, goals, and difficulties in order to deal with current problems). The remaining types are: transmissive, of cultural heritage; escapist, glorifying the past and belittling the present; obsessive; and simple narrative.

Bromley (1990) suggests that it is necessary to distinguish reminiscence, as a normal psychological process, from the repetitive and disjointed rambling of someone who is confused, with a failing memory; and also from ruminating (a morbid preoccupation with negative images and experiences from the past). Although this is a well-advised reminder, in practice the reminiscence and review of normal individuals can from time to time be shot through with rambling or rumination.

Reminiscence is adaptive, helping with the assimilation of new experience, promoting stability and consistency in behaviour. Turning memories over in the mind as a reverie can lead to: reliving pleasures; going over what might have been; rehearsing how future actions might be different from the past; and understanding past events in new ways.

Bringing memories out into the light of day by talking with others can lead to: achieving consensus by sharing experience; explanation and self-justification; self-assertion; and expressing bottled-up emotions. Bromley (1990) identifies reminiscence as crucial for psychotherapy's aim of improving the client's adjustment through reshaping thoughts and feelings. However, he is pessimistic about extending this to old age, seeing little prospect of a radical reappraisal of one's personal history in late life.

Avoidance of reminiscing can be adaptive or defensive in later life (Coleman, 1986). Coleman's detailed review of fifty people (age range 68–92) living alone in sheltered housing in the London area showed that, while twenty-one indicated that memories were valued and reminiscence was significant in their lives, the remainder either looked back on their lives as unworthy and unacceptable, actively avoiding reminiscence, or (for a variety of reasons) saw reminiscence as irrelevant for them.

His case studies reveal some subjects who provide life-history information but show little or no inclination to reflect on it or elaborate

PRO	CON
Each life has worth	Some worth more than others
Everyone wants to find meaning	There is no meaning
Sense of community with others	Sense of distance from others
Hindsight heals the past	Past poisons the present
Highlights resources	Spotlights deficits

Figure 2 Pros and cons of review

their reactions to the largely factual account they provided. Among explanations that he considers are: having led a relatively satisfying life one may experience no need to think back; and remaining feelings of grief, anger or guilt over past events are rendered less disturbing by choosing to reminisce less often.

Molinari and Reichlin (1984–5) distinguish three types of reminiscence: storytelling; evaluating experience; and defensive (against an unsatisfying present). Confining review to the second category and registering the possibility of conflict if unresolved failures, disappointments or losses are encountered, they recommend that a more circumscribed and workable version of Butler's life review is needed for its validity to be on a sound footing.

Review and psychological well-being

Review is more systematic than reminiscence. It tends to occur when people are faced with making crucial decisions about the future – for example, when illness or unemployment calls for readjustment, when a child has left home, or when retirement is getting close. It constructs and reconstrues, putting events into perspective, or rethinking the past in order to deal with the future more effectively. In later life, when the future appears foreshortened, the process is more concerned with finding personal significance in and satisfaction with the story that one has put together to represent one's life.

Review can take many forms. It can be sporadic and without deep involvement. It can be a deliberate attempt to change a lifestyle. It can be harnessed to produce a memoir – a tangible autobiography. It can be adapted in counselling or psychotherapy for an individual needing to readjust his or her life, and is of particular significance in terms of preparation for dying.

Review therapy 'started under the auspices of several converging and influential theories' (Kastenbaum, 1987, p. 324). Kastenbaum lists these as: the epigenetic conception of Erikson, suggesting that the older person needs to achieve an integrity of self by coming to grips with the actual life that has been lived; the ideas of Jung (1959), that people strive for a 'completeness of being' that requires the ability to integrate opposing but complementary tendencies within the self; and the view of Butler that review is a naturally occurring universal mental process, adaptive in later life.

Kastenbaum comments that review therapy was seen as offering an alternative to the then prevailing notion of age as a process of relentless deterioration. It was more attractive for some professionals in the field of ageing to think of it as part of life span development, in which every phase had its positive role to play. Review moved quickly from concept to putative fact, and gathered momentum to become one of the more popular approaches to psychosocial treatment.

Review has (rarely acknowledged) parallels with the process of individuation in Jungian psychology. Movement in the second half of life is said to reach behind the individual's social front to establish a self more securely rooted in past experience, using active imagination to explore and understand resulting thoughts and feelings. The objective is to transcend the pressures of unthinking social conformity and mindless unconscious fear. It is described as a bridge to psychological maturity by balancing extroversion and introversion, conscious and unconscious, action and reflection. In the second half of life attention turns inward to find meaning and wholeness that make acceptance of death possible.

However, review cannot be assumed to automatically enhance psychological well-being. It needs to be tested (Merriam, 1993); and Bornat (1994) and Haight and Webster (1995) have been among those who have attempted to focus critical analysis on its usefulness. Knight (1996a,b) presents the therapist's viewpoint.

Issues of rationale for engaging in review will be explored in Chapter 2, 'Why review?'.

Chapter 2

Why review?

SUMMARY Although reasons for engaging in review tend to be taken for granted, they should be critically appraised, as review is a personally taxing and labour-intensive process. Here they are considered under five headings: Curiosity ('hello, what's this?'); Self-presentation ('this is where it's at'); Taking stock ('how am I doing?'); Assessment ('getting to know you'); Support ('help me if you can').

This chapter examines the reasons for choosing to review. Why do people engage in review, as a listener or narrator; and under what circumstances would it be strategic to choose not to do so?

While the literature has given these questions some attention, a thorough examination is overdue. Review and related approaches consume substantial time and attention, both in the secular and religious activities of ordinary life, and in specialised settings of health and social care and therapy. In its more intense applications review can be emotionally draining and open up painful and distressing topics. It takes a relatively long time to explore a personal narrative in detail, and it is not easy to evaluate the outcome of this effort (see Chapter 8).

It must be recognised that an individual does not have to have a reason to review his or her life. A background process of self-monitoring can slip into the foreground unbidden. Examples can be cited readily – Proust's 'remembrance of things past' called up by the taste of a *madeleine* dipped in tea; or the memories of a former lover evoked by a 'cigarette that bears a lipstick's traces', from the song 'These Foolish Things'. Random cues can trigger reflection and review, taking the individual on a surprise excursion down memory lane. However, there are a number of reasons for engaging in review, and in any individual case more than one of these may be in operation at any one time. As motivation is likely to affect process and outcome, the various rationales that have been put forward need a closer look if the end product is to be better understood.

Lacking in much of the literature is appraisal of the range of reasons that can be put forward for taking part, whether as narrator or listener. This is understandable because everyday review can occur spontaneously without apparent deliberation. It is intrinsically interesting, and intuitively it appears to make sense that human beings constantly engaged in complex information processing should need to pause from time to time for an overview of what is happening to them, and how they are interacting with others.

Still, the question that titles this chapter remains an important one that demands answers. Without these, the reader will end up in an impasse similar to that described in the H.G. Wells story 'The Food of the Gods'. Wells envisages a tribe of giants feared and shunned by the rest of humankind. Towards the end of the tale, a solitary giant is described talking to himself, repeating: 'What's it all for? What's it all *for*?'

One might well ask the same question of reminiscence. Does reminiscence cause psychological health? In its various guises it can function as a pastime, as a form of self-therapy, or as part of a review shared with a therapist. Reasons for engaging in review can be grouped under five categories. A brief introduction to these follows, and they are described in detail in the remainder of this chapter.

Curiosity ('hello, what's this?')

Expression of spontaneous curiosity, surprise, puzzlement, or an emotional swing in either direction – happiness or sadness – can trigger review. This need not amount to a life crisis, but is usually described in terms of an episode of heightened awareness, an expansive moment in a constricted life. The person concerned, in an effort to make sense of an unusual happening, looks more closely at current experience, and review may be engaged at least briefly and impressions stored for future reference.

Self-presentation ('this is where it's at')

'I said to her – and she said to me' descriptions from everyday life can offer an example of self-presentation. Another is the conversation launched in a park or a pub or at a party by a stranger who opens up their story under the cloak of anonymity. Community mental health teams have co-opted and trained as listeners bar staff and hairdressers, among others, in recognition of the fact that certain social settings foster personal self-disclosure.

Self is presented in the form of an anecdote dealing with an episode or episodes from a life, or even a relatively full life story. This can apply not only to an individual but also to a couple, family, or other group. The narrator or narrators are concerned to give an account of self or selves in relation to others, as a statement of identity, and in some cases to justify actions. In the absence of listeners, a statement may be an internal monologue or a speech to oneself in the form of a soliloquy – it need not be addressed to others. Expression, then, may be through internal reflection, some relatively private medium such as a diary or a letter, or in the public domain as a speech, written prospectus, article, or book. The listener, if there is one, may be an acquaintance, new or old, a friend, a partner, a fellow-member of the narrator's group, a researcher, an oral historian, a biographer, or a member of the public if the message is addressed 'to whom it may concern'.

Taking stock ('how am I doing?')

This is different from the previous category, in that it introduces an element of social comparison. There is a taking stock of progress at a particular time where review seems appropriate – an anniversary, a developmental milestone, a point of transition, or a life crisis; and an element of evaluation in comparison with others, and checking against expectations. Expression could be as above, but this is closer to an annual report than a prospectus, and any written statement is likely to be in short form. The range of possible listeners would be as above, excluding the biographer.

Assessment ('getting to know you')

An individual, couple or group, and a listener or listeners come together. The listener has a professional purpose in wanting to hear a story in order to understand the narrator and the group to which the narrator belongs. The listener may be investigating oral history or carrying out some other form of social research; or they may be a health or social care worker getting to know a referral. The narrator may be someone who has access to an area or an era of general life experience that interests the listener; or they may be considered to have health or social problems and may be required to give an account of them in the context of their experience.

This form of review may also be done with disadvantaged groups in order to elicit information in the absence of any clearly defined problem. Target populations may include older adults, people who have learning disability, and members of other minority groups. Expression is normally through interview. The listener can be a trainee, carer, professional, researcher, or writer. Listener may become narrator: in training exercises for health and social care staff a trainee may be required to take the role of a disadvantaged client and write a first-person narrative of the client's life from the client's perspective.

Support ('help me if you can')

This occurs when an individual, couple or group has begun to engage in review, is not happy with what is emerging, or has got stuck with the process, and self-refers or is referred to a carer, counsellor, therapist' or other consultant for joint working. Expression, with formulation and reformulation of diagnosis, is likely to be through a variety of media – professionals' reports, biographical submissions, interviews, assessment techniques and tests, and audio and video recordings of communication. Listeners will be professionals, and their trainees where appropriate, and the clients are also likely to act as listeners some of the time.

If in a group, they will hear other voices telling their versions of the story, they will hear the professionals tell sections of the story to test their understanding, and they will have access to feedback from the tapes. Such approaches are commonly used in family therapy, with circular questioning and a supervisor or a reflecting team observing the process and then meeting the therapist or therapists, and often the families as well, to give and receive feedback.

Why not to review

Review is not to be recommended for everyone. Individuals or groups who have difficulty in shifting the focus of their attention tend to find review too much of a struggle. People with marked intellectual impairment – for example, dementia sufferers – can reminisce, but have extreme difficulty in linking past and present. People who feel much worse in the course of self-initiated reminiscence – putting self in the dock with the rest of the world as judge, jury, and witnesses for the prosecution – should be encouraged to refrain, or to engage the services of a counsellor or therapist as an advocate.

Kastenbaum (1987) cautions: 'among those disposed toward self-reflection, there are some with an obsessive turn of mind. Although well intentioned, we may be intensifying the problems of an obsessive older person by encouraging the LR process' (p. 325). The severely depressed dwell on the darker side of life and are disinclined to explore the light. Those who are fixated on their physical state see life review as irrelevant, as the following scenario suggests.

Scenario 3

Ivor, a 72-year-old resident in a sheltered housing complex, spends most of his time writhing, lying on his bed or on floors in his neighbours' apartments. He is convinced he has 'a trapped nerve' in his back that is causing him constant pain. Various therapies, both conventional and complementary, have not changed the picture. A psychiatrist has diagnosed depression: treatment has been unsuccessful.

Jim, who manages the complex, knows that Ivor, a former caretaker and odd job man who has lived locally for many years, has a long history of 'being on the sick'. Driven by complaints from the residents, and believing that a clue must lie in Ivor's past, Jim starts life review. Initially Ivor is co-operative and prepared to talk about early life in Wales and his success as a sportsman. Then he becomes restive, repeatedly insisting: 'My life? If you want to know about that, it's in my medical notes. Just look at those – that's all you have to do!'

- **What do you think Ivor means?**
- **In Jim's position, what would you do? (And why?)**

(See Chapter 9, p. 145.)

Curiosity

Narrators can find review intrinsically satisfying, apart from any gain in perceived control over one's own life or greater understanding of self in relation to others. Younger storytellers have commented that it feels like 'dressing down for the weekend', while older narrators have noted that it feels like putting on old slippers and automatically becoming more comfortable and relaxed about oneself.

Others report a heady sensation like putting on dancing shoes to 'strut your stuff' – occasionally such narrators are liable to break into song during review or illustrate their feelings with dance steps 'because it needs more than words'. This is akin to the enjoyment described by Kiernat (1983), discussing group work in which members identifying themselves as having had an impoverished childhood are encouraged to use reminiscence to enhance their appreciation of the present. It also relates to a sense of life as thrilling, as evoked by Lewis and Butler (1974), describing the experience of 'elementality' in review: 'The lively capacity to live in the present may be fostered through the enjoyment of people, nature, colours, love, humour, and beauty in any form' (p. 168). Excited narrators report: 'I felt as though I was there'; or 'It's as though it only happened yesterday.'

Narration confers power. Witness the wise women and wizards who relate stories and propound riddles, the *Ancient Mariner* of Coleridge, and the sailor pointing out to sea in the painting *The Boyhood of Raleigh.* Social anthropologists have indicated that across a wide range of cultures the status of older people is positively related to the amount of worthwhile information they have to share.

In emphasising the narrator's storytelling and arranging and rearranging of meaning as the core of the therapeutic process, review therapy with other reminiscence-based activities has the characteristic of empowering individuals on the basis of their experience.

Self-presentation

Researchers in life span development, marital and family studies, organisational culture, anthropology, gerontology, medical sociology, and many other areas of study, approach individuals and groups to engage them in self-presentation through biographical investigation that often taps review.

What is the point of this type of review? Three interrelated functions have been described in the literature. All relate to the narrator's subjective experience and involve enhanced feelings of: being in control of one's own life; understanding of self in relation to others; and enjoyment of life. Together with van Deurzen (1998), we conclude that people try to organise their experience to make sense. They create their own meaning, and within the limitations of existence they can be relatively flexible in revising their frameworks, in order to maintain their sense of direction and being on the right track. Review is a means to this end.

This links with Erikson's concept of the developmental task of achieving integrity, in resolution of a choice between ego integrity and despair, positive 'acceptance of one's one and only life cycle as something that had to be and by necessity allowed no substitutions', and letting go of 'if only'. Coleman (1988) is not alone in seeing that the concept of a normative life review and Erikson's developmental task of achieving integrity have a good deal in common.

Butler (1975) is dismissive of Erikson:

> His experience with the middle aged and elderly is very meagre, and his popular conceptions of generativity versus stagnation and integrity versus despair do not hold up well in my clinical and research experience with patients in middle and later life. (p. 255)

Comparing Erikson and Butler, the authors' experience suggests that each is right. We find that some narrators in later life are trying to make sense of their life as a whole, as Erikson proposes, while others, as Butler reports, are more concerned to limit their efforts to dealing with certain issues from the past that have re-emerged with ageing. If a life can be viewed as a car, it is possible to draw the analogy that some drivers opt for a comprehensive service, while others choose an inspection that deals with urgent problems.

- **Thinking point**
  Consider your experience of middle-aged and older people. What has it taught you about life review?

Butler (1963) notes habitual mirror gazing as becoming more frequent in some older adults engaged in spontaneous review. Such individuals are observed to study their reflections frequently and intensely, studying their appearance in detail. Kimmel (1990) proposes that this could represent the person actively learning to integrate a changing physical 'me' into the relatively continuous sense of 'self', in an attempt to integrate experience on the basis of current functioning.

Being alive is in itself a terminal condition, imposing urgency. An existential goal for narrators is to turn off the pressure of the information flow that is chronological time, and to review in psychological time, passing in non-linear fashion. The process may be perturbed by either internal or external influences; it may become detached from past, affirming persistence within present; and it may function in a manner unrelated to causality. Reviewing in a family context adds extra dimensions, including resonance of time shared by different generations; the currency of anecdotes, traditions, and family albums and trees; and appreciation of the developmental significance of leaving home.

In informal social encounters participants exchange information, seeking to define self in relation to other, sometimes just going through the motions, but often networking actively and exploring possibilities for moving on to intimacy. In more structured contacts, involving two-way screening with an approach to a professional individual or organisation – negotiating for advice, services or employment – biographical information is exchanged and evaluated.

Impression management in social behaviour involves the creation and projection of an image (of an individual, a family, or an organisation), and this requires the presenter to engage in regular collection, evaluation, and updating of data. Throughout such contacts participants try to lay uncertainty to rest and build up a shared narrative that is coherent – driven by a need for social respect. Attention and being noticed (without being laughed at or seeming ridiculous) are motivating factors for doing review.

Ludwig (1997) describes the art of biography, and notes that, while the biographer's ideas influence the end product, the subject is also powerful in having chosen to reveal an incomplete picture. Taking the stance of the subject, Ludwig comments:

> The story plot you follow offers a structure for your life, a vehicle for integrating your experiences, and a conceptual map to guide your way. You cling to it to keep from becoming disorientated, it becomes a *de facto* extension of you, familiar experiential territory for your life, and creates the context for your existence. This is why you try to preserve it at all costs. You may not play the prime role in composing your own personal story, but you play a decisive role in safeguarding it.
>
> (pp. 114–15)

Living through stories

Review, then, helps narrators to define their identity. 'We live in and through stories. . . . They hold us together and keep us apart. We inhabit the great stories of our culture. We live through stories. We are lived by the stories of our race and place' (Mair, 1988, p. 127).

Review gives direction to people's lives as they move towards a valued endpoint, along a well-trodden track marked by success stories – and failures. It can be consoling, helping people to realise that their experiences are normal, understandable, and shared by others, that somehow they will be able to get through.

Lewis and Butler (1974) consider that older people who use review spontaneously without a therapist or mediator are attempting to gain control of fear of approaching death. Review, they suggest, is entered as a refuge, as a person's myths of immortality and invulnerability give way. They propose that the newly vulnerable individual be understood as engaging in life review in a reflex bid to regain control.

Sometimes this represents a self-styled certificate of sanity. Edwin, an 80-year-old former journalist and now a patient in a general hospital, was terminally ill but had not yet been told his prognosis. Mistrustful and fearing the worst, he had become unusually hostile to staff and critical of their care. He was referred to a psychologist and was to review his life as 'a man of letters – an artist'. He exulted: 'This will tell those so-and-sos I'm still compos mentis.'

Like a comfort blanket, life review confers a sense of control via security. Verwoerdt (1981) points out that its purpose is not necessarily accurate recall of facts, but the weaving of edited recollections into a harmonious perspective, constructing an alternative reality compatible with self-esteem. As Nietzsche suggests, when Memory and Pride debate the re-telling of an event in a person's life story, Pride usually wins.

Indeed, Lieberman and Tobin (1983) consider that most people do not have the ability to undertake unaided the comprehensive and balanced sorting and restructuring of the past envisaged by Erikson or Jung. They see as an essential task of later life the preservation of a coherent, consistent self in the face of loss and the threat of loss. They suggest that, because human resources are so limited and the task is so pressing, review is primarily used to create an image intended to be believed, a myth to achieve a feeling of stability, justifying the narrator's life. For Lieberman and Tobin, typically, the older person becomes the protagonist in a drama that is worth telling or having lived for.

Researchers and clinicians are by no means unanimous in agreeing on the extent to which child and adolescent experiences can be understood as shaping development not only during these periods but also into adult life (Rutter and Rutter, 1992). There is some evidence that links may be traced across the life span, but this is difficult to evaluate. For example, the Childhood Experience of Care and Abuse (CECA) record provides retrospective behaviourally based information on childhood adversity. Prigerson *et al.* (1996) show that higher scores, indicating reported exposure to adverse conditions in childhood, were related to increased likelihood of having an anxiety disorder in care-giving spouses aged 60 and above.

However, use of retrospective rating has a number of problems, and the anxiety could of course have been mediated by more immediate factors. In principle, review can be used for the purpose of understanding risk factors in relation to service planning. For example, Cohler and Jenuwine (1995) use narrative method to study risk factors for late-life suicide. They gave consideration to the relative frequency of life events experienced as 'off-time' (happening unexpectedly soon or unduly late), reported by older people, and the impact of such experience on adjustment, using a psychological autopsy to understand the relative influence of cohort, period, and historical events.

In planning community care, Gearing and Coleman (1995) deployed a biographical approach to reveal how life histories had shaped current concerns of older adults, and how needs not revealed by conventional assessment methods could be matched with a broader range of services and helping strategies. Care co-ordinators gained a greater understanding of and respect for the older client; built a sense of trust, security, and acceptance with him or her; and made better decisions about the package of care and services best suited to the individual's needs.

Similar approaches have been adopted in relation to learning disabilities, in the form of 'personal futures planning' to assist individuals in developing a vision for their future and helping to make it a reality. Based on individuals' talents and skills, and not driven by limitations of services, this develops strategies to increase the likelihood that persons with disabilities will develop relationships, be part of community life, and develop competencies. A personal profile is drawn up to supply information about background, experiences, critical life events, family relationships, health, and community ties. Family futures planning, engaging friends, relatives, and professionals, may also be carried out.

Taking stock

In *War and Peace* Tolstoy describes a thoughtful and tender look on the face of Prince Andrei. Travelling to join the defence of Russia against Napoleon, the Prince is reviewing his past and plans for the future. Tolstoy comments that, when starting a journey or changing their mode of life, men capable of reflection are generally in a serious frame of mind.

Review may be done relatively frequently within a normal life in the course of general self-monitoring, or it may be done in a specific area of functioning – career progress, for example – to confirm that one is on target, without necessarily changing behaviour. If one can identify aspirations and assess levels of competence, one can identify what one wants to learn. Education and learning can be seen in the context of what has come to be called life planning or mid-career planning – a major self-assessment, often undertaken in middle adulthood.

Self-assessment involves examining one's own history of work, family and interpersonal relationships, values, interests, and priorities. Educational needs and interests emerge naturally as pointers to desired outcomes. One may come to the decision to put less energy or more energy into a vocation – or to change vocations. Each alternative usually reveals an educational need, such as learning for a new kind of job or job upgrading, or learning for the purpose of self-expression and enjoyment.

Steps in an ensuing career change process would be:

1 Self-awareness and career awareness developed.
2 Plans formulated.
3 Education pursued.
4 Job seeking undertaken and placement achieved.

Another way in which the question 'how am I doing?' may be asked is for the narrator to compare his or her story's current themes with those appearing in the narratives of peers, to determine age-appropriateness. This has links with the work of Gould (1980), who examined irrational assumptions originating in childhood, continuing through into adult experience, and found to be characteristic of particular developmental eras. For example: late teens, early twenties: 'I will always belong to my parents and believe in their world.' Twenties: 'Doing it their [parents'] way with will-power and perseverance will probably bring results. But when I become too frustrated, confused or tired, or am simply unable to cope, they will step in and show me the way.' Late twenties, early thirties: 'Life is simple and controllable. There are no significant coexisting contradictory forces within me.'

Thirty-five to fifty: 'There is no evil or death in the world. The sinister has been expelled.'

Gould's studies are unusual in the attention they give to articulating that questioning and putting aside established assumptions may be seen as a major issue in psychological development. It is not necessarily the case that the above assumptions – part of an extensive list reported by Gould as emerging from his experience as a group therapist with Californian clients from a wide age range – would be found today in a different culture.

Facing challenge

The question 'how am I doing?' may also be confronted when facing challenge of major upheaval in living. A crisis of explanation and a desperate search for solutions open up for individuals confronting extinction. For example, patients with a life-threatening illness struggle to make sense of what is unfolding for them. To simply understand the disease process, or to go through processes of 'putting your life in order' may not be enough.

Narrative reconstruction is undertaken, unifying interpretation of the present in the context of the past, trying to understand why the illness is happening now, and what could have led up to it. The narrator facing an imminent series of losses needs to do grief work – and terminal care services are increasingly offering a range of options. These include not only professionals or volunteers who can listen, but in some cases writers in residence to advise patients on how to frame the account they may feel an urgent need to prepare, not only for their own enlightenment, but also to leave a testament for significant others.

Coleman (1988) underlines the importance of 'tidying up', suggesting that in parallel with a need to settle financial affairs there may be a related concern to edit a personal narrative so that it gives an orderly presentation of a life well lived.

Assessment

The shift to community care has opened up the lives of institutionalised people to assessment, and life histories have been used successfully to promote an improved self-image for children who have spent much of their life in institutional settings. Some middle-aged or older adults have been able to tell a life story for the first time, as a maturing individual, with a unique past, separate from those with whom they may have been obliged to live for many years.

Also, in the community, a number of minority groups each have to make a strong case for their share of scarce public resources. Demands to be heard with more attention are coming from older adults and their representatives. This is attributable to the growing proportion of older people in Western society facing the inevitability of ageing (Twining, 1996). These issues become more pressing with the growth of living generations, and with multigenerational families becoming more common, with as many as four or five generations coexisting at one time, caught up in complex cross-generation issues (Hargrave and Hanna, 1997).

Under this heading there are a number of interrelated specific purposes for undertaking review with individuals (especially with the more needy and neglected ones) from this group.

Advocacy

Reviewing health care decisions, Aumann and Cole (1991) present the case of a patient aged 91 with Alzheimer's disease, using different voices with metaphor of a 'life song' to create a unified picture of the patient and her life, complete with themes, counter-themes, and harmony. Through the help of her niece, who conveyed information the patient couldn't express, the reality of the patient's life was described through the medium of family photographs with accompanying narrative. The aim of this intervention, which was achieved, was to help her doctor make an informed judgement as to what the patient would or would not have wanted had she been able to express wishes in respect of her care. On or before admission of such patients to continuing care settings, preparation of 'life books', put together in consultation with patient, family, and friends, is to be recommended.

Educating carers

Open University courses such as 'Caring for Older People' encourage students to listen to voices of disadvantaged older people speaking for themselves about their present needs and past lives. In various formats – printed, video, audio cassette – such teaching on behalf of the client attempts to change the perspective of carers so that they will appreciate the client as a person, rather than as a passive recipient of care, and accordingly will accompany personal and nursing care with human interaction, as the following example illustrates.

Tom, a new care assistant in a nursing home, is helping Claire, a staff nurse, to dress Maggie, a resident since the home opened. He is focusing on the physical task to the exclusion of consulting Maggie about what is happening. Claire draws his attention to a bedside photograph of Maggie at 21, and to watercolours showing her to have been an accomplished artist. He is at first incredulous, then recognises: 'So she was someone once, wasn't she?'

Claire addresses the patient by way of reply: 'Maggie, you still are someone, and it's all right for Tom to talk to you, isn't it?'

Maggie nods.

Enhancing quality of life

All care for people in later life is, or should be, directed towards achieving 'wholeness', so that they can actively enjoy, and not simply have to endure, life (Bright, 1997). In residential settings orientation sessions improve levels of communication between carers and old people. This is particularly relevant for those with language and/or memory impairment. It constitutes a way in for prospective key workers, it can bridge transition to new settings, and it promotes advocacy. In the course of review, the narrator begins to 'feel someone', that is, to be noticed and valued.

Promoting understanding

Incomprehensible 'challenging' behaviour can be reinterpreted. For example, a woman who insisted on carrying her possessions around at all times was found to have spent the first forty years of her life in institutional settings without private space.

Another who kept wrapping any clothes she could find in a bundle that she carried with her everywhere she went was found to have yielded, more than thirty years before, to family pressure to give up her baby for adoption.

Tapping an information resource

The older adult is a repository of personal information that can become lost. This may exist in oral form, but when a family carer dies, or a paid carer moves on, it is likely to be dissipated. Having it tapped and recorded in a life book may be used to strengthen a caring relationship, such as the one described below.

Scenario 4
A mother and daughter are referred as being in chronic conflict with each other by a carer support organisation, to Judy, a counsellor. At 68, after a series of strokes related to a history of alcohol abuse, Margaret is separated from her husband and living with her carer Jane, 30, divorced with two small children.

Margaret introduces Jane not as 'my daughter' but as 'my remembrancer'. Margaret explains that her memory is impaired and she depends on her daughter for prompting. The daughter confirms this as the main source of conflict. She adds that her mother had been a high-flier in the Civil Service who had seen little of her only child until she was forced into early retirement, but that she is now 'making up for lost time'.

Her mother agrees and refers to her half-finished autobiography which she keeps in 'the box', a lockable tin file in which she had formerly kept her most important papers. When completed, this would explain everything, but she doubts her ability to finish it.

- **Why might Judy suggest that the couple engage in review?**
- **How might Margaret and Jane use it?**

(See Chapter 9, p. 146.)

Support

In using review for therapeutic support, two main interrelated functions can be identified. These are: jointly working out a life plan to be implemented to effect change; and enabling, again through cooperative effort, the client to feel sufficiently positive and in control of their present and anticipated future, so that any plan can be put into action with a reasonable hope of success.

Making a plan

Life planning can involve counselling, including exercises to clarify present values and aspirations, to identify blocks to achieving goals, and desirable personal changes to be worked towards. Sugarman

(1996) describes implications of a life span developmental perspective for counselling practice.

Developmental problems in a client's life are likely to require review. If an articulated developmental goal is lacking, the personal narrative will not be coherent, and within the counselling process the narrator will feel fragmented. If, mistakenly, there is a disease perspective rather than a developmental perspective on life events, disruptive life events may be avoided strenuously, and if encountered will be reacted to as diseases to be fought and dismissed as quickly as possible. Counsellor and client will need to appreciate that change and upheaval are par for the (life) course. Reluctance to let go of the past, or present, can be confronted. The counsellor can help the client to become aware of the age-graded expectations of society, and to create personal goals, while understanding that deviation from age-graded expectations is to be undertaken consciously. Both need to be aware of likely consequences.

Knight (1996a) makes the point that, even if we do not concede that there are typical developmental changes in adult life, we could consider review as taking in the learning of age-graded roles rather than personality change as such. Learning of this kind required in the normal course of adult development could in itself be problematic and stressful.

Inadequate management of earlier developmental tasks may well become an issue for counselling. As development is cumulative, present problems may result from inadequate or incomplete resolution of tasks. Developmental issues may have been by-passed or may need reworking. The client who is deficient in change management skills may not have recognised that regular change is necessary in the course of development. Help may be required with transition management, goal-setting, action planning, and implementation, using associated techniques of brainstorming, analysis of the pattern of pressures and opportunities faced by an individual, and prioritising.

Control

An important 'why' for the counsellor or therapist is assisting the narrator to feel in control of life (as far as this is possible in an uncertain world). This ties in with a theme developed by Goldfarb and Turner (1953), concerning the urgency of understanding the need of patients, particularly those in middle or later life, to feel powerful and in control during the process of psychotherapy administered by a younger professional.

We feel validated and empowered as narrators, McLeod (1997) points out, and he describes use of power as one of the most important themes in counselling. Coping methods, which have worked in the past, can be rediscovered; reality orientation and a bridge to the present can be created; and incentives for change can be established. Paradoxically, letting go of concern for power may strengthen a narrator's sense of control (Magee, 1991b).

For the more frail narrators, letting go of past activities and relationships may become a key objective (Waters, 1990). In areas of society where mourning rituals are rare, discussion about death is virtually taboo, and lack of expression of grief is perceived as coping well, a listener may usefully review with mourners the life and relationships of the person who has died. The focus would be on helping mourners to begin to accept the reality of loss, to experience pain or grief, to adjust to an environment in which the lost person is missing, and to reinvest emotional energy in new relationships.

Brink (1979) describes the importance for a narrator of feeling in control of the process of living, and considers that review, when it is helpful, is helpful because it reminds the narrator that life is a series of crises and protracted struggles. Through persevering, success has been achieved. Such an interpretation serves as a powerful motivation to cope with new demands of the present. When the listener debriefs the narrator on the story that has been told, it is essential to emphasise enthusiastically this interpretation of the story.

Lewis and Butler (1974) link review with Jung's individuation process. As Jacobi (1968) explains, Jung's main interest in this was directed to the second half of life, which he saw as an opportunity for initiation into an inner reality, developing a deeper self-knowledge by giving attention to concerns and traits that had been neglected and hidden from awareness.

Lewis and Butler argue that those engaged in review reflect in order to resolve, reorganise and reintegrate what is troubling or preoccupying them. They suggest that a listening therapist would facilitate the narrator's ongoing reflections, making them more conscious, deliberate, and efficient, supporting rather than supplanting what is happening. Edinberg (1985) appears to agree, advising that review should be developed around whatever type of analysis of previous events the narrator is doing.

Self-defeating life stories have to be understood and re-written where possible. More likely to be at risk are women, ethnic minorities, the mentally ill, and older adults. There is a need for self-empowering stories (Viney, 1993) which remind the narrator that the efforts that have been made by them and by others on their behalf have not been without reward, and that, when one is swimming against the tide, not having been swept away is an achievement in itself.

As Garland and Garland (1995) point out, a subjective sense of being in control is also important for carers of individuals suffering from disabling conditions such as a dementing illness. They describe selective use of brief episodic life review in order to reframe problematic events for a dementia sufferer and, more particularly, for the carers. The purpose is to alter the meaning that an individual or a group attaches to certain interactions, making a situation more amenable to change. Carers are persuaded to explore alternative ways of viewing and responding to the behaviour of a demented person, through the medium of a closer understanding of their shared life experience, and the way in which that experience shapes the individual's attempts to cope. Review can restore a sense of control to depressed narrators, by enabling them to bring up experiences that challenge all-or-none assumptions.

Scenario 5

At 74, Blodwen is convinced that nothing good has ever happened in her life. She is being treated for depression in a psychiatric unit with a care plan to 'resocialise' and 'remotivate' her. When Helen, a nurse, asks her if she knows what these terms mean, the patient looks blank but eventually hazards a guess: 'It means they want me to take two of the yellow pills instead of one . . .'

When review starts, Blodwen has difficulty in recalling anything positive, but Helen persists and together they go back sixty-six years. Blodwen acknowledges that when she was 8 her parents had a corner shop in Cardiff, open all hours, and one Saturday night were celebrating a good week's receipts. They gave her a few pence to get some fish and chips for herself – a rare treat. She called for 'my friend – she had a squint and she was smelly, but she was my friend' – they got the fish and chips and shared it in the rain under a street light. And they were happy.

- **How could Helen and Blodwen develop this dialogue?**
- **How could this relate to Blodwen's treatment?**

(See Chapter 9, p. 147.)

Conclusions

The five categories of motivation – curiosity, self-presentation, taking stock, assessment, and support – are not mutually exclusive. Assessment and support tend to go hand in hand when the listener is a health or social care professional, and the other categories are unlikely to be absent, although they will have varying influence according to the topic under review and the stage the review process has reached.

In everyday review, although curiosity is the wellspring of all activity, it is difficult to sustain without the added incentives of needing to communicate to others through self-presentation, and the individual's need to take stock by self-monitoring progress across the tasks and stages of development throughout the life span.

Because review is a taxing process that makes heavy demands on listener and narrator, it is necessary to tap all five sources of incentive in a creative and flexible way, moving from one to another and neglecting none.

- **Thinking point**
  At this point, consider your experience to date in reviewing your own life. Why have you engaged in it? You have probably chosen to impose limits on your review. What do you think you might discover about yourself and others if you were to choose to proceed beyond these limits?

Chapter 3 will deal with 'Structure, scope, and status' of review.

Chapter 3

Structure, scope, and status

SUMMARY The structure of review (how it is put together) includes recognition of readiness, exploring and interpreting life events, shaping time, and planning for the future. Review can be involved in: everyday reminiscence; autobiography and biography; oral history; life span development; career planning; counselling; family therapy; and individual psychotherapy. Its status in use by health and social care professionals is examined, with consideration of ethical issues of informed consent, autonomy and competence, ground rules of biography, and authenticity and personal values.

Structure

Review has been defined in Chapter 1 and its challenges outlined. What follows is a more detailed picture of what it involves. Subsequent chapters deal with how it functions, its practice, outcomes and their evaluation. Most stories have a structure with beginning, middle, and an anticipated end. While an individual episode of review can be fragmentary and formless, the overall structure of the life of an individual or a group is no exception to this general principle of being constrained by form.

The process starts with a narrator's readiness to engage, which may be spontaneous, or emerge as a continuing effort linked with awareness of approaching dissolution and death. The starting points of review can come in the form of repeated statements such as: 'my problem is . . .'; 'we can't go on this way'; 'I don't see a way out of this'; 'it must be me. Is it me?'; 'I saw something nasty in the woodshed'; and many more. Or they can appear as untoward behaviour that is so disproportionate to the situation in which it is being expressed that an explanation is sought: 'Just what is it that has led this person to react in this way?'

Life events

The substance of review is the exploration of life events and their cognitive representation. A key feature of form is content, which can be operationalised as number of past events identified by individuals, and their evaluation of them (De Vries and Watt, 1996). In De Vries and Watt's study of men and women across the life span, the average number of significant life events recalled is fourteen, with a range of one to thirty-five. Older people recall a significantly greater number of events, and women recall significantly more than men do.

- **Thinking point**
  How would you account for these differences?

The most frequently identified events are: moving (relocation and migration); marriage or the start of a relationship; schooling, including beginning and ending; and career landmarks, including starting work, major career change, and retirement. Other events often chosen are illness, injury, family milestones, and episodes of personal development involving fresh insights (including therapy experiences). There are also a number of relatively unusual events – ending piano lessons, writing a book, having an abortion, becoming a vegetarian, and coming out sexually.

De Vries and Watt note that, overall, 71 per cent of outcomes are regarded as desirable, 16 per cent as undesirable, with the remainder being seen as both desirable and undesirable. This could reflect a general tendency for individuals to remember more successes than failures and more good than bad personal experiences. There is a general tendency for people to perceive themselves as being effective in getting what they want out of life.

The primary dimensions of life events appear to be: undesirability, event magnitude or intensity, uncontrollability, and unpredictability. Undesirability appears to be the most crucial, and is linked to psychological disturbance; major life events have been found to occur more frequently in the immediate histories of clinically depressed patients; and uncontrollability is also associated with psychological disturbance over events for which the individual was not responsible, or which typically could not have been prevented. Perceived pleasantness/

unpleasantness of a life event can also be linked to the extent to which the event was anticipated, and the extent to which adjustment was possible.

Interpretations

Reminiscing about events is often accompanied by the narrator's explicit or implicit interpretations. Typically, narrators develop from one to three dominant themes in a pattern that is stable over time. The themes may be classified as validating (confirming that the person has lived a worthwhile life), or lamenting (negative interpretations of past events). Validating themes are: positive self-appraisals; having had the opportunity to make choices; having had positive social contacts; having had experiences that were interesting, joyous, or unique; and depreciating the past in comparison with the present. Lamenting themes are: regrets; having lacked choice; and having had difficulties.

De Vries and Watt see structure as integrative complexity, an information-processing variable assessing the cognitive structure underlying thought. Analysing their respondents' stories paragraph by paragraph they score each recollection of an event on a continuum. At one end is a lack of differentiation, with a categorical, all-or-nothing approach to information processing, or the perception of only a single acceptable perspective or dimension. At the other is high integration and differentiation, with multiple embedded levels of schemata (patterns for classifying situations).

Joe, a trainee psychologist, is trying hard to assess the troubled relationship of a young couple. He decides to elicit the personal constructs of each partner. The woman produces a complex yet clear pattern of ways of thinking and feeling about relationships and situations, which is coherent and enables her to discriminate between shades of meaning.

The man is more limited: almost every judgement about people or events revolves around 'likes football/doesn't like football', or 'to do with football/not to do with football'. Joe is driven to depart from the conventions of this form of assessment and actively suggests other constructs that his client might want to try, but his efforts are unavailing.

- **Thinking point**
  In Joe's place what action might you have taken in response to this undifferentiated narrative?

Shaping time

Review is also shaped by time, and is a way of shaping time. Boscolo and Bertrando (1993) propose a time lens, recognising the importance of co-ordinating different times. They suggest that people who feel stuck in their lives often see time in a linear-causal way: past determines the present, and the present leads inexorably into the future. The therapist's task is to introduce a reflexive relationship among the three dimensions of time – what we define as the reflexive loop of past, present and future – making time for hypothetical pasts and futures in the present.

Age-linked roles are among the markers that structure review. As mentioned in Chapter 1, social roles are age-graded. Increasingly, a family sequence is a complex procession of these, likely to involve breaking-up and re-forming: dating, living together, child rearing, splitting up, separation, another relationship, blending one or more family groups. The significance of clocks as metaphor for our development should be underlined.

With the ticking of the biological clock, markers of ageing influence the way we feel about ourselves, because of their socially defined meaning as reminders that time is running out, and as precursors of the approaching end of life. The cohort clock tells when different groups entered the stream of historical time, and this is an important source of perceived differences between individuals. Cohort differences in values, taste, beliefs, and attitudes can be striking. Differences may be seen not as the results of growing older, but as stemming from experiences which younger people have not had.

It is important to understand a narrator's life in terms of what was normative for their age group or cohort, not for the listener's if you are from a different cohort. At the same time one should not necessarily expect to support all the values of the cohort, and it may be necessary to be prepared to point out that these are not rules that must be followed for ever.

Scenario 6

At 53, Morag, who never married, has been living alone in the family home for ten years. At one time she had shared the house with her mother, who died at 70. Morag cared for her mother, an invalid, for more than twenty years. As Bill, a 28-year-old community psychiatric nurse, listens to her review, which she tends to present in a similar form to anyone who will listen, he forms the impression that she still feels bitter at having been required to sacrifice her life to look after her mother. When he shares this impression she becomes angry.

Mother, says Morag, repeatedly told her that she should go off to make her own life, but at the same time communicated the expectation that her duty was to stay. In telling her story she insists that her listener is 'too young to know' what she is talking about when she refers to a sense of duty formed in a childhood 'back in the nineteen-fifties when everything was different'.

- **From the perspective of your cohort, what would you understand by 'a sense of duty'?**
- **What expectations would you have for yourself if you were to face a similar challenge?**
- **In Bill's place how would you reply?**
- **What more would you want to know about Morag's story?**

(See Chapter 9, p. 148.)

Where are you within your family structure? The narrator's answer to this question determines how old they feel, how alone they feel, and what kind of issues regarding maturity are to be dealt with. Families have unfolding stories across the successive generations, and a narrator's place in (or outside of) that story has important implications for their self-concept.

The future

For Knight (1996a), reviews are never complete when they are finished; and he points out that as well as the past and its relevance for the present, it is necessary to consider the narrator's scenario for the future. Older adults are less likely than the young or middle-aged to expect improvement in the future: in general they see it as likely to be negative or stable. If time is known to be limited, in the presence of life-threatening illness, deciding on what unfinished business should have priority is an issue of greater urgency – calling for more therapeutic commitment and energy.

People in general tend not to plan post-retirement lifestyle in detail. Retirement lengthens, we spend more time in the child–parent relationship as adults than we do as children, widowhood is a predictable role for women, and most of us will be frail for a few years prior to death. Knight (1996b) concludes that we might choose to resolve our early conflicts with parents differently if we realised that we would be connected with our parents for more decades in the future than the two spent as their child. A daughter-in-law might be treated differently if viewed as a likely future caregiver. We could give more thought to post-retirement life in which we may spend two or three decades.

Scope

Review is used across a range of human activities. The following selection includes some of the more obvious areas, but it is not a catalogue.

Everyday reminiscence

This is not the preserve of older adults. Review comes with self-awareness. It is not limited to middle or late life, although much of the research to address this process directly seems to make that assumption. Lowenthal *et al.* (1975) find that approximately 14 per cent of students, 33 per cent of newlyweds, 44 per cent of middle-aged parents, and 12 per cent of people approaching retirement are engaged in review. From early childhood we confront the questions: 'Who am I?' and 'How do I fit, in the world around me?' We answer these by creating personal myths, McAdams (1997) concludes. We are the stories we tell.

For older adults, Moody (1984) notes the importance of reminiscence in the regeneration of the public world. Considering the concept of generation in relation to adult life span development, he describes reminiscence as the working through of the past of an entire generation. A continuity framework for reminiscence is adopted by Parker (1995), presenting it as a reflexive process through which individuals introspectively define themselves with the main objective of monitoring their life course and avoiding – or at least anticipating and preparing for – major deviations.

Reminiscence has to fit in with the exigencies of everyday living. For example, surviving on a rubbish tip in Mexico City and scavenging to stay alive demand preoccupation with the present's minute-to-minute struggling. This could call for a moratorium, perhaps a permanent one, on reflecting on past experience, even considering the prospect that this might lead to realising one's full potential through self-actualisation (Maslow, 1970). As Maslow suggests, for most people in most situations human needs are organised in a hierarchy so that physiological needs, essential for the body's survival, and safety needs, generally have priority.

However, to remember this is not to suggest that reminiscence is a luxury denied to poor people. Sumerlin and Bundrick (1996) use a forty-item brief index of self-actualisation, including life meaning and purpose, to compare American males who had completed college education, with males who had some college education, but who were unsheltered and homeless at the time of the survey. While the former score higher on two of the seven factors – core self-actualisation and democratic character – they are not significantly superior on life meaning and purpose, or on openness to experience. (Possibly the homeless men felt sustained by the American Dream – the belief that even if present circumstances are unpromising, with sufficient enterprise and hard work success can be achieved.)

Autobiography and biography

Studying life review in 149 narrators, males and females aged from 11 to 85, Labouvie-Vief *et al.* (1995) find that mature adults move from representations of self that are relatively poorly differentiated from others or social conventions, to ones that emphasise process, context, and individuality. The scores for development of a differentiated self peak in middle age, and are lowest in preadolescents, and in older adults. Not all cultures, though, would see this as an indicator of psychological maturity. Eastern psychology asserts that ego differentiation is the basis of all conflict; and an undifferentiated state of being allows for the development of a complete and harmonious personality (Nitis, 1989).

Guided autobiography (Birren and Deutchman, 1991) in a group format, generally with older adults, has as its principal themes: account of major branching or choice points; family; life work; health; sexual identity and behaviour; money; loves and hates; and experiences with death and dying. Over a minimum of ten two-hour meetings each member each time offers a two-page story on the set topic, and these are discussed and generalisations are framed by the group and facilitators who participate in the exercises.

For Birren (1987), review puts us in touch with 'the best of all stories'. He contends that this process puts the contradictions, paradoxes, and ambivalence of life into perspective, restoring our sense of self-sufficiency and personal identity. Describing his intensive courses on guided autobiography – meeting three hours a day over two weeks – he comments:

> The most important thing I have learned confirms Hemingway's observation that 'the world breaks everyone and afterward many are strong at the broken places'.
>
> I tell each of my classes, 'You are all survivors. Tell us your story and we will tell you ours.' I don't tell them how strong I think they are, since that is part of the process of individual discovery. In reviewing the details of their lives people become impressed with all the problems they have survived, and the many ways they have been tested by events and by people.
>
> (Birren, 1987, pp. 91–2)

Frankl (1985) would agree. He points out:

> In fact, the opportunities to fulfil a meaning are affected by the irreversibility of our lives. But also the potentialities alone are so affected. For as soon as we have used an opportunity and actualised a potential meaning, we have done so once and for all. We have rescued it into the past where it has been safely delivered and deposited in the past. Nothing is irretrievably lost, but rather, on the contrary, everything is irrevocably stored and treasured.
>
> (p. 175)

- **Thinking point**
  Reflect on a challenging situation that you have come through. What have you gained from this experience?

Connection between meaning and biography is basic, in the sense that what people find meaningful about themselves and their world is expressed through metaphors, stories, narratives, and autobiographies. Stories are the way the world is for us. A life story does not contain the answer to something – it is the answer. It has components of feelings and wishes. An authentic life story is the one that a person imbues with meaning.

A biographical approach may facilitate acceptance of one's life experience but this may well fall short of achieving ego integrity, wisdom, and a coherent model for general understanding of the meaning of life. It would be invidious to quote examples but ex-politicians' life stories rarely reveal that much of lasting significance has been learned by the narrator.

At the end of a life review there may simply be the general reaction, 'that was real', or a recognition, 'yes, that's me'. We may seek meaning, but that does not necessarily mean that the stories we are need to add up in the end, that our lives must be seen to fit into a grand narrative. A final story may be provisionally titled 'Work in progress'.

Oral history

Two main uses of oral history can be distinguished. The first is as an academic and research activity that gathers material from 'ordinary' participants in activities and events of social life. Recent oral history conferences have dealt with topics such as cinema, health, sport, religion, migration, and the lives of women. Oral history can also be used as a basis for projects within communities on their recent history and how this relates to issues in the present: these may be used to educate, empower, and entertain those taking part.

Oral history involves the recording of people's memories on audio- and videotape. It gives voices to the 'silent majority' of modern history, enabling them to put on record their experiences and those of their families and communities. Myths, legends, songs, children's rhymes, poems and plays held in memory, parables, and tales of the supernatural, carry history. The Australian aborigines only have an oral history. Nothing was written down. There were people who were the keepers of these stories and responsible for passing them on.

Storytelling is an existential phenomenon stemming from the basic propensity of a human being to create and discover meaning (Kenyon, 1995). The principle is to listen to and accept the story of another, a story that is 'ours in the making', and to enable the other to continue on their journey and find their own direction. In the course of life review conducted as a component of counselling or psychotherapy, participants often describe the social fabric of their lives going back over the years. While such accounts should not be dismissed, the listener in these circumstances needs to be persistent in repeatedly drawing the narrator to consider how history has shaped the present. Both should appreciate that they are operating within a medium of living history, and that conclusions reached long ago need to remain open to questioning and reappraisal.

Life span development

Developmental studies use review to elicit from subjects at different ages and stages their experience both within their reference group and in comparison with members of other groups. Review is recognised as a continuing process that can be sampled at different points in time. Precisely how is review to be distinguished from other uses of the past? Selected themes of mourning and caring, and integrity, have been dealt with in review groups including low-income women aged 65–85 (Silver, 1995).

Career planning

The role of review in vocational guidance and planning career choice and change is increasingly being developed with the emergence of the 'coach'. This life-skills consultant uses life review as a tool to help a client identify changes that can be made in personal and professional lifestyle.

Michael, who is 29, works long hours in a city office as a legal consultant with a company providing services to business. The company, in common with its customers, is of necessity profit-driven, and while Michael enjoys what he does he feels a general lack of sympathy with its end product, which he sees as: 'Adding profit for companies who've already got more money than they know what to do with.'

In his scarce spare time he has Green interests, particularly in small-scale permaculture (the development of agricultural systems intended to be sustainable and self-sufficient). He thinks of downshifting, moving to the country to become self-employed or to start a co-operative enterprise. Frustrated by his own lack of progress in realising his ideal, he seeks the advice of a 'coach'.

- **Thinking point**
  In Michael's position what life issues might you want to review with the 'coach'?

Counselling

Review is more likely to be successful in an interpersonal context, and positive outcome is associated with initial unhappiness in the client (Silver, 1995). Payne (2000) sees the narrative approach as fundamental for counsellors in assisting the client to describe the problem with a wider perspective that can be expected to be more likely to generate solutions. Counsellors of many schools would share the view of Clarkson (1999) that (from the viewpoint of Gestalt) the counsellor needs to be committed to lifelong growth and personal development in order to be authentic in encouraging clients to develop their potential.

Family therapy

Families may be asked to engage in a review of the collective 'life' of the family system. Byng-Hall (1995) defines family scripts as the family's shared expectations of how family roles are to be performed within various contexts. That is, anticipation of what is to be said and done within family relationships, as well as family pressures to perform the roles as expected.

Scripts are represented by scenarios which are repeated patterns of typical interaction recognised as significant for family relationships, and include: a context in which family members engage with each other, for example, getting together to celebrate an anniversary; a plot, in which members' motives emerge in the course of time; and an outcome, in which consequences of the scenario emerge. These scenarios may be viewed in therapy as attempted solutions to the family's difficulties. When each scenario comes up for review in therapy there are always subtle variations – developments and unexpected consequences to be reported.

This focuses the therapy on how the family can do things differently. Family members come to believe that they can change things for themselves. Some scenarios are enacted within the session, which allows the therapist to be involved in some of the fresh moves, and assist in improvising new solutions.

Individual psychotherapy

The Adlerian concept of focusing on eliciting early recollections in detail, because they are taken as important indicators of the developmental track that an individual is liable to follow, may offer a quicker and possibly more productive way of facilitating ego integrity in late maturity than conducting a life review beginning with the present and working back (Sweeney and Myers, 1986). Review has been used in healing trauma in Holocaust survivors and others for whom traumatic memories have re-emerged in later life (Hunt *et al.*, 1997).

Reminiscence can be satisfying in itself. Review therapy builds on reminiscence in three ways. Therapist and client are committed to personal growth; the ensuing process gives particular attention to conflict resolution and the continuing evolution of coping strategies; and as therapy progresses client and therapist note they are not where they started. The client has become more like the person he or she really is, as outgrown defences have been examined, found wanting, and laid aside. Between reminiscence and life review therapy, is life review, where reminiscence is related to the present in an effort at self-evaluation akin to a form of self-therapy. The very processes that Butler (1963) viewed as characteristic of review – reminiscence, thinking about oneself, reconsideration of previous experiences and their meanings, and mirror gazing – can be found in psychotherapy.

Does this mean that a therapist facing a client who is ready to launch a review can expect that the groundwork for a therapeutic alliance will be in place? That the therapist could say with assurance, 'not only am I boarding a moving bus, but my client the driver and I will be in agreement on the route and destination'? This is not necessarily the case, as we shall see in examining the concept of review, and the range of its therapeutic and other functions. Review is a pervasive theme in psychotherapies, which work towards a client's achieving 'insight' in developing a more varied and useful set of models for the interpretation and understanding of experience. Most therapies bring in some elements of review as a component of understanding oneself and effecting change in unresolved conflicts.

Status

Moody (1988) reviews literature on twenty-five years of review practice. He sees most of the studies as appearing to weave a collective myth comprising a hopeful – perhaps even rosy – view of later life. While understanding that gerontologists would be attracted by the notion of researching personal renewal, he cautions that life history methods may become over-stretched. He is uneasy about a tendency towards widespread application of such approaches across a wide range of topics, such as the study of transmission of social and cultural expectations across generations, or socio-political analysis of rights and responsibilities of older people in society.

It is understandable that health and social care professionals were excited in 1963 when Butler reaffirmed the significance of review. Dobrof (1984) recalls: 'In a profound sense, Butler's writings liberated both the old and the nurses, doctors and social workers: the old were free to remember. . . . And we were free to listen, and treat rememberers and remembrance with the respect they deserved' (p. xviii). Kastenbaum (1987) comments that one of the attractions of review is to offer a positive side to ageing, in a culture where reflection tends to be undervalued and thought of as positively un-American. At the same time, he warns, advocates of review have tended to press its advantages with over-hasty enthusiasm.

Reservations

A number of commentators have expressed reservations about over-enthusiastic application of the term 'life review'. Knight (1996b) notes that the phrase has become a buzzword. It covers too many activities, from simple suggestions that it is all right to reminisce, through the intermediate suggestion that the professional listen to the story and attempt to understand what is said, right up to psychotherapeutic intervention. Karpf (1982) sees the approach as supportive rather than interpretative, and comments that, while the optimism of Butler and his colleagues is infectious, it strays away from what many would consider psychotherapy to be.

Edinberg (1985) agrees that, while review therapy encourages clients to 'get their life in order' and is a flexible approach that can be tailored to individual or group, it must be criticised for: lack of clarity on how to apply procedures; over-reliance on clinical judgement of how to use it; little scientific validity; limited utility in handling specific problems (such as adapting to organic impairment); and lack of clarity about how this therapy might benefit persons with reactive depression, or how it might conflict with other therapies. Kastenbaum warns that, when professionals have the best of intentions and find beguiling concepts close to hand, they should sharpen critical attention to basic assumptions and differential applications. Their urge to find and apply positive techniques can overwhelm the need to examine what they are doing.

Ethical issues

In assessing the status of any procedure it is necessary to be concerned with practical ethics. Reflective reasoning attempts to answer the question: 'What should I do in this situation, all things considered?' It deals with action concerned with our own or other people's lives, and involves decision-making taking into account the interests of all persons directly or indirectly involved in a situation or affected by a course of action. The phrase 'all things considered' epitomises practical ethics. Ethical reasoning requires putting oneself into another's place to see a larger picture beyond self-interest.

Informed consent relating to research and intervention

In qualitative research the consent process can become a lengthy negotiation between researcher and subjects, rather than a formal moment when a consent document is signed. Mutual trust is needed so that the researcher can get from the narrator information that may be intimate. There is an obligation to make sure that the narrator is not harmed and that the privileged access will not be misused.

It involves rights to privacy and confidentiality for the narrator. The listener's responsibility is to ensure these, and to bear in mind others involved in the story. Social research promises anonymity for respondents: in practice, gathering detailed individual stories may violate this. This is a serious ethical issue, since narrators are often relating episodes from their life stories (dealing with, for example, intimate relationships) that may never have been disclosed to another person.

While written consent for future use of biographical materials is recommended, not all potential uses may be known to begin with. If a new use arose – for example, if the researcher wanted to publish material on the Internet – the researcher would have an ethical obligation to contact narrators before publication. Right to privacy implies that individuals have control over when and how information about them is passed on; and confidentiality indicates that access to private information has been limited by agreement.

How does the notion of informed consent apply to persons whose competence and decision-making capacity are open to doubt? On the one hand it is unethical to rule out such persons from being interviewed. On the other, the person's capacity to make an informed decision on taking part needs to be assessed directly. The listener needs to have recourse to consent from the narrator's family or other responsible agents if assessment proves negative.

Such assessment may not be welcomed by the interviewee since some of the questions may provoke alarm ('what's this all about?') or anticipation of being found wanting ('it's a long time since I was at school . . .'). Risk-benefit analysis, done indirectly without engaging the narrator, gives only part of the picture. As informed consent needs to be truly voluntary, the listener will need to allow ample time for discussing with respondents the implications of their decisions.

Autonomy and competence

In what contexts is biography a prerequisite for ethically informed intervention? When do people have a right to have someone listen to their story? All persons are stories, are still creating stories, and have a story to tell. The dementing or otherwise frail individual is not a face without a story, and has a right to be heard. If they are not heard in this way they may make themselves known in more disturbing ways. Halberg (1990) shows that listening to their stories and responding appropriately could significantly reduce excess noise-making in severely demented patients. In the course of such a change in responding to the patient, the carers' own vocational stories would also be likely to change for the better.

Ground rules of biography

The narrator comes first. The ethics of storytelling and listening should be seen from the viewpoint of the narrator. The basic assumptions and purposes of various approaches and programmes need to be clarified and respected with regard to both training and implementation. For example, a biographical review may be used primarily as therapy or primarily as education or recreation. In either case the purpose needs to be clear and listeners need proper training and supervision.

Self-awareness is important for the listener, who needs to reflect carefully to clarify the extent to which constructing or reaffirming the narrator's own story might get in the way of listening. Self-awareness needs to be developed, as the listener brings assumptions and personal as well as professional stories to the biographical encounter. In the ring, as it were, from the professional's point of view, there is my personal story, your personal story, my professional story, your story as a client, and the story being co-created in the situation encompassing all of these. In such a crowded contest one cannot guarantee a safe and easy resolution.

The more relevant information the listener or reader possesses, the more open, flexible, and genuinely interested they can be. A biographical approach increases the possibility of bridging the gap of subjectivity, and entering the experience of the narrator. Problems arise when others (family, friends, carers, and the listener) simultaneously are making the narrator's experiences into a story in a way that distorts. Nevertheless, interdependence within family and community characterises life stories, and with frail and dependent narrators the need becomes stronger to establish a story that balances requiring the help of others and being able to negotiate on what terms help is to be given and received.

Universality

Is review a universal phenomenon? Self-reflection is a basic human capacity, but should everyone be pressed to engage in this on mental health grounds? Coleman (1986) indicates that some individuals do not choose to reminisce and do not appear to suffer as a result; and Webster (1993) considers that depression, recent trauma, and even traits such as obsessionality could be contra-indicators for biography-based intervention, which could be experienced as invasive and inappropriate.

Authenticity and personal values

What can one expect from a life story? First, it will to some extent be opaque and incomplete. A story is from a particular point of view that changes with experience and the telling. The narrator cannot and does not see or know all there is to know. The process of narration is in mid-story, and neither narrator nor listener can be sure how it will end as the plot thickens. It is not possible to arrive at the final truth about a life. We do not know the origin of events, or have a complete understanding of what we can and should hold ourselves responsible for. Secondly, we are not one story but a collection of stories. In private, semi-private and public dimensions there are tangles of tales – economic, physical, family, emotional, and cultural, among others. It is unlikely that all will fit tidily into one overarching narrative.

Wallace (1992) asks people to 'just tell their story'. The results are anecdotes related in a specific interpersonal context – ready-made 'life stories' are not told. We are part of stories that often do not easily blend into overall coherence, and which can appear to signify, if not nothing, then at most nothing in particular. We cannot become any story we want or change the plot at will. We do not know which parts of our story are programmed or locked in, and which are open to the possibility of escape. Authenticity does not mean true or genuine as opposed to false. None of the characters has the entire script. A healthy share of humour and detachment may be the best response to the stories we are. Improvisations continue, and to demand a satisfying beginning, middle, and end may not reflect an accurate description of coherence.

Conclusions

While some of the main components of review can and should be separated out, it is not possible in the present state of knowledge to be much more specific in setting out its structure. Indeed it may be unrewarding to do so: in the telling American analogy it would be like 'trying to nail jelly to a tree'.

Review itself appears to be a component of at least eight activities, and this wide scope needs to be recognised in order to understand the challenges of engaging in it. While health and social care professionals have on the whole welcomed its development, some have understandable reservations about it being deployed in an over-hasty way. Review makes a number of ethical demands that need to be grasped.

Chapter 4, 'How it works', considers the active ingredients of review.

Chapter 4

How it works

SUMMARY Positive one-to-one attention, encouraging the narrator to express emotions, and comprehensive coverage of the life span are key variables contributing to review's effectiveness. Active ingredients are positive reinforcement, letting go, acceptance, insight, reframing, control, and commitment to progress. A preliminary model for how these may interact in practice is discussed. There is potential for being more explicit in identifying and using such factors.

It is not easy to get a clear picture of how review operates, or to know what its active ingredients are and how these can most usefully be refined and combined. The topic lacks conceptual clarity, as reminiscence and review do not readily lend themselves to definition. However, in psychology and related disciplines enough is known about how people appraise their experience and approach new learning for it to be possible to offer a clearer understanding of how review works than has been the case up to now.

Review is after all widely accepted as a psychological reality of everyday life. It is grist to the mill for researchers (a topic to investigate), teachers (a theme for transmitting their ideas), and practitioners (a tool to extend their practice). There is evidence (see Chapter 8) that review is effective in increasing psychological well-being.

Integrating concepts from therapeutic approaches that tap reminiscence in different ways, this chapter summarises components of review that could make it effective in maintaining well-being or in producing positive psychological change. It is acknowledged that these components are not mutually exclusive, that this is not an exhaustive list, and that their relative importance will vary from narrative to narrative. A preliminary model for how these are likely to interact will be described.

In the literature on applied reminiscence, there are general summaries of beneficial factors said to be intrinsic to the concept of review. For example, Sherman (1981), explaining the use of reminiscence in integrative counselling, highlights three factors. Used supportively, it enables the client to: identify with past achievements and positive events, so as to *enhance self-esteem* and fortify the self-concept; dispute retrospective generalisations, the negative distortions of the past which make for much of the despair, working through rational disputation and changing the way the client attributes responsibility (teaching the client to stop attributing all the blame to self); and use *self-re-evaluation*, by applying new standards of self-evaluation to old situations brought up in review.

Perhaps as a consequence of general acceptance in the literature of review as being on the whole 'a good thing', relatively little effort appears to have been expended on investigating and comparing the variables in the process, to discover how it operates. Haight and Dias (1992) are unusual in attempting to identify key variables that make reminiscing more effective. In a study of older adults in nursing homes and sheltered housing, comparing ten reminiscing formats, they came up with three factors related to positive outcome. These are: individuality, or a one-to-one situation; evaluation, with the narrator being actively encouraged to express feelings at key points in the story; and structure (a schedule of topics to work through, covering the whole life span).

Individuality is seen as providing the narrator with the privacy to recall and examine life events, including those too personal to discuss in a group, and enabling their narrative to have a listener's undivided attention and feedback. Evaluation is described as narrator and listener talking about how they feel and what they think about life's incidents. For instance, one subject talked about her joy at receiving a phone call from her first love. The evaluative listener asked such questions as: And how did you feel? Were you happy? Did you cry? Why did you cry?

Haight and Dias define evaluation as an aspect of therapy that occurs in reminiscing. Use of the evaluation component requires skill, and, although they advocate the use of review by paraprofessionals, they insist that evaluation must be used with care, because it can take the listener into therapeutic territory. They see review as essentially different from psychotherapy.

They use an earthy metaphor: in review the listener helps the narrator to wrap up life's garbage and take it out; but in psychotherapy, the listener helps the narrator to search through the garbage looking for its meaning, and only after this is finished is the garbage taken out or recycled. This analogy sounds ill-chosen, but appears to be offered not to signal disrespect for the content of stories and how narrators and listeners deal with them, but primarily to emphasise the distinction that Haight and her co-workers seek to draw between review as therapeutic listening, and psychotherapy proper.

The crucial difference is said to be that the therapeutic listener discusses only issues raised by the narrator. Often, the therapeutic listener recognises that the narrator appears to need to discuss a particular period of life, but specific issues are not discussed unless raised by the narrator. This is a puzzling distinction since it would appear to conflict with the fact that in Haight's preferred interview format the listener is active in cueing the narrator to cover all periods of life, and in prompting the expression of emotion in reaction to recall of life events.

Structure is not discussed in depth by Haight and Dias, who agree that it has two main results – it brings order and it assures recall of all developmental phases. Which of the two is the more important remains uncertain.

A model

This chapter will look at actual and potential factors contributing to understanding what could be happening in review to effect change, examining some of the major contributions to the debate, and suggesting how these appear to operate and how they might be related to each other. It is important to remember that review is a continuing process that occurs in a variety of formats across a number of contexts, and that the activity can be spasmodic, with many intervals of quiescence or regression. In such circumstances it is not possible to be prescriptive, setting out rules for how review should function.

In Chapter 1 three modes of review are identified. Mode 1 is relatively unstructured and unspecific, self-generated in everyday life; Mode 2 is semi-structured and more specific, more characteristic of reminiscence group work in community and residential settings; and Mode 3, relatively more structured and specific than the first two, is most often found in the context of counselling or therapy. These are considered in more detail in Chapter 6.

Our observation of and discussion with narrators we have worked with over the last eight years lead us to propose that there is a

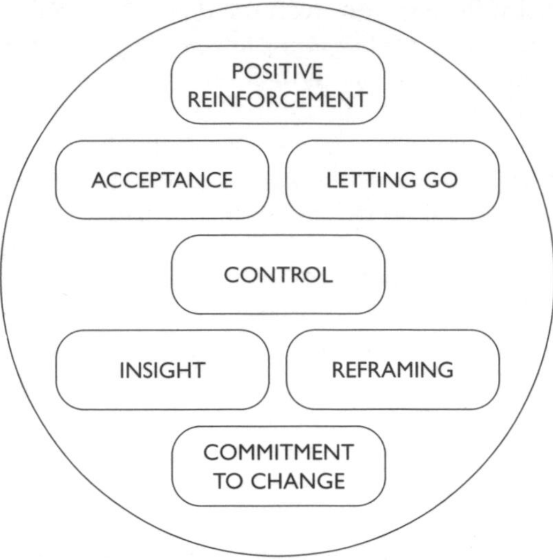

Figure 3 Review factors

five-step sequence underpinning review. First, its continuance is contingent on the activity being found positively reinforcing by the narrator, who finds valued consequences from engaging in it, in any mode. Secondly, the narrator will seek to balance acceptance of memories that are retained, and letting go of memories that are no longer required.

Thirdly, achieving a broadly successful balancing act of this kind can be expected to result in a subjective awareness of feeling more in control of one's life. While the second and third steps can be made in Mode 1, they are more likely to be achieved in Mode 2, because the semi-structured and more specific approach, with more consistent supervision and group support, increases opportunity for progress of this kind.

Fourthly, the narrator who gains greater insight into how life has been lived, and options that remain, is enabled to translate this into reframing perception of what has happened, is happening, and could come about in the future. Fifthly, if commitment to change can be established in a context of support for graded experiments with change in thoughts, feelings, and behaviour, then insight can trigger action in the way the narrator's life is enacted.

While these latter steps may be achieved in Mode 1 in exceptional circumstances, and can sometimes be made in Mode 2, they are more characteristic of Mode 3, since this can be expected to provide the most structured and specific learning opportunities.

Sources

Among the sources that have been drawn on in developing the above model are: research on autobiographical memory, human judgement and decision-making, and life span development; and description of self-awareness, and contemplation and meditation (secular as well as religious). Also to be tapped is the thinking of therapeutic schools, including: cognitive behavioural therapy, existential counselling, Gestalt therapy, neurolinguistic programming, personal construct psychotherapy, Progoff Journal Workshops (Progoff, 1975), the Quadrinity Process (Hoffman, 1988), rational emotive therapy, and transactional analysis.

Each of these has links with review, and in some cases review in all but name is integral to their practice, so that the key factors they identify have in a sense pre-empted efforts yet to be made by review practitioners to answer the question 'how does it work?' It needs to be remembered that the setting in which review is done and the personal attention of the facilitator or facilitators who may be present are important in their own right.

For example, describing the Journal Workshop approach, Progoff compares it to the eye of a hurricane, at the centre of life, a free, unconditioned moment of opportunity, and a sheltered situation safe from the outer pressures of the world, in which the narrator can quietly reappraise a life.

Positive reinforcement

There is widespread recognition that review well applied can be intrinsically a source of positive reinforcement for the narrator, if only because for each of us to think and talk about ourself is a fascinating topic. Also, reminiscence is not just self-centred: to share one's story with others in groups meeting in everyday life is to increase investment in the community, through naming, caring, linking, asking for help, trusting others more, and experiencing less distress. In extreme circumstances, where a person is caught up in a process or system which threatens individuality, the self-affirming effects of review are of special importance. It is, for example, valued in care of the dying, and hospice patients have been supported in life review to affirm uniqueness and sense of self-worth.

Techniques for tapping 'remembered wellness' to improve well-being in the present are described by Benson (1996) as drawing on reminiscence. To elicit the relaxation response, he teaches patients to focus on something that pleases. He tells them it doesn't matter if that is a tape of forest sounds, a postcard of a beach they went to last summer, a piece of paper on which an inspiring phrase is printed, the smell of incense they recall from church, or the feel of their trainers on the pavement as they jog.

Benson asks them to focus in ways that feel natural to them. Such visualisation often targets a very soothing, beautiful place they have been to on holiday, or some comforting place they remember from childhood. He also encourages them to use affirmation, a brief message or phrase to repeat to themselves, in order to introduce a new sensory idea to a brain accustomed to a stream of negative thoughts or self-criticisms.

Julie, a psychiatric patient recovering from an episode of severe depression, is in her early thirties. She has a striking antique ring, which her counsellor, Leah, admires and asks about. Julie comments wanly: 'They tell me it's diamonds and sapphires . . .'

Leah responds to this unusual phrasing, asking: 'And what do you think?' Julie does not reply, and begins to sort through her jewel box.

- **Thinking point**
  How might you take this up in review, as a listener?

Bender *et al.* (1998) believe that shared reminiscence is more likely to recur if the results are intellectual and social stimulation, a feeling of having left behind a cultural legacy – footprints in sands of time and a sense of having achieved intergenerational communication.

Webster (1993) reports development of a 43-item Reminiscence Function Scale, from a 54-item prototype measure. A total of 710 adults (aged from 17 to 91, mean age 45) completed the latter, with results being submitted to a principal components analysis. The author identified seven major factors: boredom reduction; death preparation; identity/problem solving; conversation; intimacy maintenance; bitterness revival; and teach/inform.

Scattered throughout the literature are recurrent references to narrators variously reporting feelings of enhanced control of their own lives, insight into their own and others' feelings and behaviour, and enjoyment of living, but little or nothing appears to have been written on how these overlap, or on their relative priority in different situations.

Verwoerdt (1981), though, notes that a two-dimensional model may go some way towards describing what goes on in review. He describes an account of a self-chosen twelve-month retreat in the mountains by a 65-year-old man who wrote down his thoughts and impressions from day to day. At first, the journal was a convergent 'vertical' record of autobiographical material demanding concentration, memory, and logical thought. Then, gradually, 'horizontal' impressionistic thoughts reflecting fleeting observations, playful and using free association, began to emerge, and during the final six months became more dominant.

In some phases of review, assurance of being in control of one's own life is the salient issue: responsibility, intention, self-efficacy, and purpose are elaborated. In effect, the narrator declares: 'I may be stubborn . . . difficult . . . bloody-minded . . . but I am not going to be pushed around . . . taken for granted . . . just used by other people.' In this mode, strategic thinking dominates: 'I thought to myself . . . I made up my mind . . . it was time for me to have a say in what happened.'

In other phases the narrator turns to expressing a wish to reflect on and understand the action around them in terms of feelings and their implications for self-esteem and relationships. Expression at these times tends to be more discursive and fragmentary: 'It sank in then . . . I got the message . . . it really hit me . . . so that's what it's all about.'

These phases tend to alternate within sessions like contrasting segments of a Gestalt pattern in which 'figure' and 'ground' vie for attention. The narrator (or listener) who becomes fixated on the issue of decision-making and taking charge of one's own life may well risk premature termination, settling for being safe rather than sorry. If the search for understanding self in relation to others becomes the object of fixation, the narrator (or listener) can become overly concerned with exploring feelings and lose sight of other action. Flexible movement between and balance among these alternates is required.

Letting go

People are attached to frames of reference that give meaning to their everyday activity. Even when unexpected circumstances intervene they cling to what they know. Sometimes this tendency is tragic-comic.

A businessman stepping into the street and thinking about his latest deal does not see the car until it is too late. A Good Samaritan takes off his own coat and pillows the victim's head while waiting for an ambulance. Suddenly the victim opens his eyes and looks around in understandable puzzlement. In relief, the Samaritan blurts the first thing that comes into his head: 'Are you comfortable?'

The businessman focuses his gaze with an effort. His answer comes readily. 'Well, I wouldn't say comfortable. But I make a living.'

Release from harmful assumptions and outdated ideas, 'beginning with a clean sheet', is the main goal for some narrators, who recognise in review a paring down which can rid them of psychological clutter. Describing the literature on creative writing as a form of psychological healing, DeSalvo (1999) says that traumatic events that have become topics for such writing include: loss of home, violence, racism, homophobia, anti-Semitism, rape, political persecution, incest, loss, and illness. She cites Virginia Woolf who acknowledged that her 'novels' were in fact elegies, each being written to try to recover something or someone she had lost.

Many religions have formalised this process. For example, Catholics who successfully practise the daily Examen of scrutinising one's relationships with others and with God, set out in the Ignatian spiritual exercises (Alphonso, 1990), are said to find that issues become no longer problematic. Failings are not eliminated – they are still a part of the individual, but they fall into place and are integrated.

In terms of personal construct theory, counselling involves a process of reconstruction to bring about desired changes in the clients' views of themselves and their worlds (Fransella and Dalton, 2000). Part of this process is selective loosening of construing, coming to question and change established ideas which are restricting ability to cope in a flexible way with present situations. The authors caution that this can be hazardous because loosening is about giving up control, and our ability to test out and predict events. They warn that the client who is clinging to his reality by holding his construing under a tight rein can easily be faced with a chaos, should an over-zealous counsellor insist on loosening at all costs.

Transactional analysts hypothesise that an important factor operating in the construction of human life plans is a programming system, the *script apparatus.* For Berne (1974), a prerequisite for *intimacy* (engaging with others in an open and spontaneous way) is for the person to get rid of accumulated mental rubbish. He argues that each of us, under parental pressure in early childhood, forms a preconscious life plan or *script*, usually based on childlike illusions, which may persist through a whole lifetime. In the course of development, given favourable circumstances, it is possible that these illusions dissolve one by one, as life crises are resolved, so that we become unscripted.

For those who remain stuck in their script, the possibility of *internal release* (freeing oneself) remains; or the original parental *injunction* (prohibition or negative command) can be contradicted by an *antithesis*, a therapeutic intervention which contradicts the injunction. For example, an adult individual still enacting a 'be a good girl' script could get the message 'now you're a woman' from the therapist. This gives her *permission* to disobey the injunction, to bring about temporary or permanent release from the script's demands. In this formulation life review therapy can be viewed as a means of analysing a script or its vestiges, in order to achieve independent age-appropriate behaviour.

The separation theory described by Firestone (1997) is similar, in focusing on breaking dependency bonds built up in childhood. His approach is called voice therapy because it brings internalised negative thought processes to the surface with accompanying affect in a dialogue format, such that an individual can confront aspects of his personality that feel alien.

One technique that is used is to ask patients to verbalise their negative thoughts *toward* themselves in the second person, 'you' as though they were talking to themselves, instead of 'I' statements *about* themselves. Statements such as 'I'm a failure, I can't succeed' become '*You're* a failure. *You're* never going to make it.' As soon as this method is employed, Firestone claims, strong feeling is released as patients give vent to thoughts and feelings indicating an intensity of self-contempt and animosity toward self of which they were previously unaware.

Ryle (1997) describes the importance of *reformulation* for cognitive analytic therapy (CAT). This is a shared enterprise of building up a picture of the patient's life, with special attention to dilemmas (mistaken belief that choice can only be made between polarised options), traps (negative self-fulfilling prophecies), and snags (being pressured into giving up appropriate goals). A draft summary is gone over in the fourth session, acknowledging the reality of what does not appear to be in the power of the patient to change, and setting goals for therapy.

Ryle explains that most of the contents of this summary will have been discussed in the sessions, but maintains that hearing the linked account, with its attempted clarification of inappropriate guilt and denied responsibilities, and receiving an empathic account of their life experience, usually have a powerful impact on patients.

Pennebaker (1997) notes that expressing emotions appears to protect the body against damaging internal stresses, and seems to have long-term health benefits. He proposes that the long-term effect of inhibiting traumatic memories acts as an ongoing stressor and undermines immune system functioning, with a consequent liability to increased incidence of physical illness.

Asking why suppressing problems appears to take a toll on health, and how buried trauma could affect the immune system, he discusses how writing about problems could affect health, healing old emotional wounds. He cautions on risks of self-disclosure; and advises on how to know who to trust as a listener.

The reduction of death anxiety has been described as perhaps the most important aspect of letting go in older adults, and Fishman (1992) reports that practice of review has negative correlation with death anxiety. Frankl (1973, pp. 91–4) gives a noteworthy example of effective use of review with a depressed patient in terminal care.

Acceptance

For Haight *et al.* (1995) the goal of review is to help older people reach integrity in a six-week process. They use Erikson's definition – 'the acceptance of one's one and only life cycle as something that had to be and of necessity permitted no substitutions' – while leaving open the question of whether integrity can most usefully be regarded as an end state, an ongoing process, or an achievement that with increasing life span may need to be re-established repeatedly in later years.

Integration may take place across separate lives led by one individual. An example is presented by Galassie (1991), of a review workshop for gay people in their fifties and sixties, to integrate within their whole life stories their sexual histories, which to some extent had been kept apart and 'under wraps' because of social pressures.

Repentance is an important issue for very many people. The Eriksonian crisis of integrity vs. despair may be compared with the Talmudic approach to death, its effect on the years preceding death, and preparation for death. Its ultimate goal, according to Spero (1981), is the gaining of wisdom through a heroic and creative act of repentance. For older people who have survived major psychological trauma such as the Holocaust, Lang and Lang (1996) describe survivors' needs to talk about the horror and assuage their guilt because they have survived. Richter (1986) looks at patients in late life facing death in a hospital setting. Connecting with cherished religious symbols, and interpreting past events as having potential for new insights, he calls for a new look at repentance and confession.

A feeling of acceptance can be achieved in review with a relatively brief recall that can be looked at in a new light and applied to the present. Mervyn in his mid-forties is surprised at the clarity with which he remembers across forty years of a life 'in silent torment', having been given a smile and a hug from a teacher when he had become distressed at school. He had been overwhelmed by this response, and to his embarrassment had become even more distressed. Other children noticed and made fun of him and he had resolved not to show his feelings in future. In accepting his own tears as that child, Mervyn goes on to become more able to accept his own feelings as an adult.

Acceptance of existential challenges appears as one of the most important healing factors in existential psychotherapy, and Yalom (1989) offers one of the clearest accounts of how this operates. He sees the most relevant 'givens' of existence as: the inevitability of death for each of us and for those we love; the freedom to make our lives as we will; our ultimate aloneness; and, finally, the absence of any obvious meaning or sense to life. Yalom points out that assuming responsibility is not synonymous with change: there are two crucial happenings in psychotherapy. These are: the patient's assumption of responsibility for his or her life predicament; and the patient's act of willing (initiated through wishing to be different, and enacted through deciding).

Letting go of selfishness may be a valued ingredient in review, particularly in cultures where the group has greater importance than the individual. There is more emphasis in childhood in China on being born into a family and placed in a network of interrelated persons. A 'little me' maintains its interdependency within the context of the 'big me' (the family, the state, the world) throughout life. This is a view of selfhood, echoing traditions of Taoism and Confucianism, as well as present-day socialism.

In the light of the health notion of psychological balance and emotional tranquillity, combined with the conception of 'big me' and 'little me', when a person is troubled in China he/she is usually advised to 'think it through' or to 'view things clearly'. The individual is expected to put things in a wider context, to view oneself in relation to the total scheme of things, exert even more self-control; and to think about the present and future rather than dwell upon the past (Dien, 1983).

Insight

The term 'insight' can sound unduly portentous, and some writers such as Masson (1988) positively dislike the term because they see it as condescending abuse of language by professionals trying to brainwash clients into seeing things their way. Egan (1998), in describing the first stage of his Skilled Helper Model, refers to eliciting a story that will reveal 'blind spots' for the client, and in turn help the client and counsellor to see where there is 'leverage for change' in formulating a new story. We use the term 'insight' to describe a shift by a narrator who comes to take a new perspective on an old story. Sometimes this realisation can be expressed as 'ah-ha' learning, a eureka experience.

Mike is a 37-year-old engineer whose life never goes as smoothly as the civil engineering projects he works on for a living. He is recounting for the fifth time a list of the reasons why he had found it difficult to get started on planning how to simplify his chaotic social life.

Patricia, his counsellor, leans forward, about to say what she had said in response to his third and fourth accounts, but Mike forestalls her. Grinning, he mimics her: 'That was then and this is now.'

Patricia nods. Mike's grin fades. Slowly, he repeats in his own voice: 'That was then . . . and this is now. That means . . .' He begins to tell for the first time a story set in the immediate future describing the life he would live.

Schema change takes place in review, according to cognitive therapists. Schemas are inferred structures (similar to personal constructs), underlying and controlling symptoms, and organising experience and behaviour. They include beliefs and rules, are largely in the realm of awareness, and in the course of therapy become even more accessible. They produce consistent bias in both judgements and attribution of meaning, and this leads to dysfunctional feelings and behaviour.

In mental health, 'schema' is applied to highly personalised structures activated during depression, anxiety, panic attacks, and obsessions, which then become dominant. Schema-focused therapy argues patients out of distortions, having them react with feeling within the session to fantasies or recollections, and identify and practise alternative thoughts, feelings, and behaviour.

The schema that 24-year-old Gordon most wants to review is 'nobody likes me'. Its roots are in his early experience of a variety of unsuccessful fosterings. Using one page for each year of his life, Gordon and his therapist Paula gather historical evidence for and against the proposition that he is totally unlikeable. It is predicted that if this schema were true there would be few items in the 'evidence against' column and an increasing number of facts in the 'evidence for' column as he grew older. Gordon discovers that evidence for his being likeable is much greater than he had imagined.

Paula also helps him to recognise alternative explanations for the evidence that had seemed to support his 'nobody likes me' schema. Appreciating that historical review in itself doesn't necessarily remove the power of a schema that he had lived most of his life building up, he moves on to begin to construct and validate a 'some people like me now, more will as they get to know me' schema.

Reframing

Payne (2000) notes that clients coming for counselling usually present a dominant story that is in the foreground of their experience and that they consider to be especially significant in explaining who they are and how they have come to be that way. Such a story is 'problem-saturated', selective in focusing on pessimism and defeat, and highly selective in omitting positive elements. It reflects unexamined assumptions embedding persons' negative views of themselves, their dilemmas, and their perceived inability to deal with challenges.

As Payne points out, the counsellor will attempt to encourage the client to modify the dominant story by deconstruction, with detailed description of actions, feelings, and thoughts over past, present, and future, to enable the person to take a different, more flexible, position in relation to the problem. In the process, circular questioning may be used to assist the client to consider how others view the situation.

The counsellor looks with the client for clues to alternative story lines, significant memories, or other elements that don't fit and even contradict the dominant story. These might include hidden strengths or personal qualities, or painful recognition that the narrator's dominant story is causing others to suffer. The objective is to enable the client to recall parallel previously hidden memories and to recognise that memories in the dominant story were incomplete or distorted. The goal is to develop a modified story to include previously neglected elements, which could be drawn on to deal with problems.

Changing patterns of self-talk may become a focus of review:

Rob, in his mid-fifties, has been troubled by OCD (obsessive-compulsive disorder) for thirty years. For the last two years he has been particularly upset by his tendency to recall and dwell on persistent vivid visual images of his wife 'laughing and joking' with others in various social situations. He is a highly introverted and possessive individual who 'knows' that the situations are innocuous, but who 'feels' with growing certainty that these images are feeding into his growing jealousy and repeated arguments with his wife. He has tried to blot the memories out, 'making my mind a blank', but this has proved impossible. Peter, a psychiatrist, tries to discover other memories, which are not negatively charged. At first Rob will only talk about his life before his marriage, twenty-five years ago. Eventually, he is able to recall that years ago on a family holiday he and his wife and their children were relaxed and happy playing with a blue frisbee on the beach.

- **Thinking point**
  How might Peter and Rob take up 'the blue frisbee' to make progress?

Challenging the dominant story is intended to produce reframing (seeing a situation in a different way and expressing a new understanding of what is happening). This gives an opportunity to transform meaning in terms of neurolinguistic programming. O'Connor and Seymour (1993) indicate possibilities inherent in looking at a situation from a variety of viewpoints to gain room to manoeuvre towards a wider range of solutions. They describe a six-step reframing process, from identifying the response to be changed, through to confirming with the individual concerned that they are completely in accord with the desirability of change.

In personal construct therapy (PCT) and counselling in a personal construct framework, one of two frequently used assessment techniques is a self-characterisation sketch written by the client in the third person (Fransella and Dalton, 2000). A step further than this, they report, is for the therapist to become aware of how the client construes his biography. They argue that, while no narrator needs be a victim of his life story, he may become a victim of how he *construes* that biography.

What does the client consider to be the most important events in his past? It is not the events that have pushed the client to where he is, but the interpretations that he has placed upon his experiences. The basic question becomes 'how does my client construe his life role?' This, Fransella and Dalton point out, needs to be answered in terms of how the client construes other people, which can be addressed by the second technique, a repertory grid to explore the client's ideas about self in relation to others.

Control

Payne sees naming the problem as being a priority for each new client to tackle at an early stage, with the assistance of the counsellor who floats possibilities until agreement is reached on a brief jargon-free definition. This, Payne suggests, encourages focus and precision in joint work. The way is cleared for relative influence questioning (White and Epson, 1990), to examine not only the influence of the problem on the life of the person, but also the influence, actual and potential, of the person on the life of the problem. A therapist may then link this with externalising (using descriptive language to enable the person to separate from the problem, and not to see it as intrinsic, caused by personality flaws).

Payne suggests that other steps that can support the client in feeling more in control of their story are 'un-membering' and 're-remembering'. In the former, the narrator is assisted to envisage presiding over 'a club of life' and to feel free to suspend or dismiss members (former abusers or ex-partners linked with memories of extreme distress) whose continued presence as characters in its story is causing grief. In the latter, the narrator is encouraged to bring in others, in imagination or literally, to witness to the validity of their new account of experience.

Because developing a radically different story can feel risky, narrators at this stage are aided to 'anchor' the new lifeline by associating it with symbols of the safe present – physical aspects of the counselling setting which contribute to their feeling secure. They are also advised to root and establish their new story by telling and re-telling it to a variety of valued others, and to seek feedback.

When therapist and client work together there is a pattern of control that influences the effectiveness of therapy, whatever the approach. This may not be politically correct to state but it should be acknowledged. Transpositional therapy, which evaluates the level of control the client is prepared to allow through choosing whether to transmit information, points out that the client remains in ultimate control (Whiteside, 1997).

The Intensive Journal process, according to Progoff, provides:

> A method by which we can each develop interior capacities strong enough to be relied upon in meeting the trials of our life. It gives us a means of private and personal discipline with which to develop our inner muscles. When we rely upon these, we are indeed self-reliant because these inner capacities are ourselves. (1975, p. 15)

Schulz and Heckhausen (1996) equate successful ageing with the development and maintenance of primary control throughout the life course, which is achieved through control-related processes that optimise selection and failure compensation functions. Selection processes regulate the choice of action goals so that diversity is maintained and positive and negative trade-offs between performance domains and life stages are taken into account. Compensation mechanisms serve to maintain and enhance competency and motivational resources after failure experiences. Both compensation and selection processes are motivated by desires for primary control, and can be characterised in terms of primary and secondary control processes.

Primary control – behaviours directed at the external environment – attempts to change the world to fit the needs and desires of the individual. Secondary controls are targeted at internal processes, and serve to minimise losses in, maintain, and expand existing levels of primary control. Secondary control helps the individual to cope with failure, and fosters primary control by channelling motivational resources toward selected goals throughout the life course. Primary control has functional primacy over secondary control. There are trade-offs as the two undergo systematic shift in response to opportunities and constraints encountered (Heckhausen and Schulz, 1995).

Resource anchoring is a therapeutic procedure from NLP (neurolinguistic programming), described by O'Connor and Seymour (1993).

It involves assisting a client in: focusing on a current situation in which he or she would like to act, feel, and respond differently; recalling experience of a resourceful state (courage, confidence, etc.) which would be most valued for dealing with the current situation; vividly and clearly recalling a specific occasion when the resource was experienced; choosing anchors (specific cues in several sensory modalities) to be associated with recall of the resource; and re-experiencing the occasion, rehearsing the cues, and identifying a precursor feature of the problem situation which can be used as a signal to trigger improved coping 'next time'.

Wong (1995) sees instrumental reminiscence as preserving a sense of mastery. He considers that, while we need to help clients to become aware of their feelings of inferiority and the self-destructive strategies they use in their attempts to overcome inferiority, we also need to encourage them to recall accomplishments and successes in achieving life goals.

Rybarczyk (1995) believes that older adults about to undergo stressful medical procedures benefit from a prior opportunity to tell their life stories. He reports success in testing his hypothesis that such preparation is a buffer against anxiety because of its mood-elevating effects, and that focusing on past accomplishments and triumphs over adversity reminds patients of their proven coping competencies and resources (see Chapter 8).

Confronting myths and counter-myths in review is a way of gaining a greater sense of control over one's own destiny. Gatz *et al.* (1983) describe myths of older women's lives seen as characterised by poverty, intellectual incompetence, illness, lack of excitement, bereavement through loss, loneliness, and sexlessness. They recognise that, while these are unduly negative in tone, they have some basis in fact; and that counter-myths describing older women as gaining in authority and autonomy are over-optimistic, and fail to acknowledge actual problems.

Guggenbuehl-Craig (1991) asserts that older people do not have to be wise. Proposing a counter-myth of the Old Fool – to balance the wise old man and woman idealised by our culture, and by Jungian, transpersonal, and New Age psychologies – he suggests that life review could help people in later life to enjoy control through idiosyncrasy.

The literature on judgement and decision-making would suggest that it is possible that as individuals progress in review they become more proficient in its practice, better able to use dialectical reasoning to draw together and integrate information into meaningful patterns. This circular process can often result in a switch in the knower's configuration of the meaning of the information set. Decisions reached through dialectical reasoning have the character of justifiable or warranted opinions. Defence of the correctness of a decision proceeds by advancing arguments that are sufficiently persuasive that the judgement is warranted.

Dreyfus and Dreyfus (1986) distinguish five levels of proficiency: the novice, who uses rules but does not make allowances for context; the advanced beginner, who is able to draw on situations already experienced as a form of context; the competent performer, who can draw on awareness of the consequences of various possible responses; the proficient performer, capable of producing a pattern of integrated actions; and the expert practitioner, who can appreciate, sometimes intuitively, the configuration of the whole situation that is being confronted.

In this formulation, therapeutic listeners use exemplar categorisation with each new narrator (sifting through an extensive collection of particular case experiences to work out how the current encounter fits in with accumulated experience). Their particularity and sensitivity to the uniqueness of each helping encounter is retained. Biographical materials have the capacity to furnish configuring patterns that integrate disparate influences on human performance. They offer local knowledge (rather than general), and show the relations between the events and happenings in a person's work with a counsellor by displaying the parts of the work as linked contributors to resolution of a life episode. Biographical materials use narrative operations to transform a list of disconnected life events into a unified story with a thematic point.

Commitment to progress

An example of moving on to experiment with different behaviour is the self-characterisation sketch mentioned earlier. Such a sketch can be the starting point for personal construct therapy. The client prepares a second sketch, not radically different but including selectively some of the desired shifts in thinking and behaviour, which have been identified in counselling. This role is then tried out as an experiment, with the counsellor's continuing support and feedback.

In transactional analysis (TA) terms, a redecisioning process is described (Stewart, 2000). This is invoked for the client who, in TA terms, is caught up in a 'racket system' – a repetitive and unproductive pattern of behaviour in adult life considered to stem from a life script laid down in consequence of one or more childhood decisions setting out 'this is how it's going to be'.

Stewart describes a comprehensive programme: contracting for a redecisioning session; the client being guided to re-experience the scene of the original decision; description of the problem then and now; re-enactment of the decision; becoming aware that the limited resources that the child had to draw on have been augmented by resources that are available to the client as an adult; taking a new decision (within the child's time-frame but informed by an adult's knowledge); affirming the new decision as an adult; anchoring (paying attention to immediate surroundings and feelings to ground the decision in the present); de-briefing to ensure the client feels fully back in the here and now; and contracting for change in adult behaviour to translate the new decision into reality.

Hoffman (1988) develops a similar theme in describing the Quadrinity Process, a therapy that makes extensive use of review. 'Each time the adult intellect attempts to make a change, the emotional child opposes; the little stubborn child within throws up obstacles, resistances, psychosomatic illnesses, excuses, lapses in memory, anything it can to defeat the best intentions for change' (p. 182). Hoffman proposes that a closing and crucial stage in the Process is for the narrator to bring the two to confront each other, in a 'bitch session', and agree to work (and play) together.

Many psychologists have identified ways of maintaining commitment in those who have undertaken review, and one of the clearest statements of how this can be done is offered by McGraw (1999), who outlines ten strategies for 'doing what works, doing what matters'. As he suggests, narrators can help themselves to keep on track by identifying guiding principles for their future behaviour that they have learned in the course of review, and by consistently self-monitoring to make sure these are applied consistently.

Chapter 5, 'Narrators and their stories', considers characteristic themes and particular concerns raised by narrators.

Review is not a rare phenomenon. People are passionately interested in self and in others, exchanging capsule life histories in a continual search for understanding. Two shoppers at a street corner are deep in conversation about a shared acquaintance. As you pass, one of them purses her lips, then delivers a considered verdict: 'Yes, she has a heart of gold but every time she opens her mouth she puts her foot in it.' Some labels for a biography may take years of careful effort to achieve – 'a safe pair of hands', for example. Others – 'a loose cannon' – may be gained in a moment of indiscretion.

Account-giving is required in many situations throughout the life span – educational screening, vocational interviewing and other selection procedures, finding a partner, legal proceedings, health and medical screening, and therapy encounters. People facing life in retirement are challenged to review in order to change perspective. Re-orientation from doing to being is required. Self is to be evaluated not in terms of function – 'what I do' – but rather in terms of 'who I am'.

Stories interweave fact and fiction. Autobiographical memory is a highly selective edited version of reality (whatever 'reality' really is). Sometimes, as in the following scenario, this editing process is laid bare unexpectedly.

Scenario 7

'The Old Salt' is a psychiatric patient in his late eighties. A former farmer, he had held the guided autobiography group at a Midlands hospital entranced with tales of the sea from his youth when he had a spell in the merchant navy. One day when Amanda his daughter makes a rare visit, Carol, the therapist, who had been reading her notes with increasing excitement, asks whether she would mind some of her father's stories being used for an article about the group. Amanda smiles: 'If you've got time for fiction! He's never seen the sea. Not once in his life! Talked about going but he had his beloved cows to look after – wouldn't trust them to anyone else.'

- **As Carol, how would you have reacted?**
- **How would this have influenced your response to 'The Old Salt' in subsequent meetings of the group?**

(See Chapter 9, p. 149.)

Although much of the literature focuses on older adults looking back over many years and coming to see pattern and meaning, a grasp of 'what it's all about' does not have to be left until later life.

Children learn that rules for living may be laid down at an early age. An adult narrator from Cape Cod Community College, Boston, told a recent conference on community education, that much of what she really needed to know about how to live, what to do, and how to be, she learned in kindergarten.

Share everything. Play fair. Don't hit people. Put things back where you found them. Clean up your own mess. Don't take things that aren't yours. Say you're sorry when you hurt somebody. Wash your hands before you eat. Flush. Warm cookies and milk are good for you. Live a balanced life. Learn some and think some and draw and paint and sing and dance and play and work every day some.

Take a nap every afternoon. When you go out into the world watch for traffic, hold hands and stick together. Be aware of wonder. Remember the little seed in the plastic cup. The roots go down and the plant goes up and nobody really knows how or why, but we all are like that. Goldfish and hamsters and white mice and even the little seed in the plastic cup – they all die. So do we. And then remember the book about Dick and Jane and the first word you learned, the biggest word of all: LOOK. Everything you know is in there somewhere. The Golden Rule and love and basic sanitation. Ecology and politics and sane living.

- **Thinking point**
  From your own early schooling experience, what did you learn about living that you would include in your narrative?

Review is not a cure-all. For both narrator and listener it is important to be selective, weighing the advantages and disadvantages of a proposed approach before reaching an informed decision. Focusing on the utility of review for older adults, Kastenbaum (1987) considers that it may not be a universal process. He points out that some people manage to have active and eventful lives without much attention to the past or the future; and he indicates that a crucial question remains: under what circumstances is review valuable, and under what circumstances is it useless or potentially harmful?

Brink (1979) suggests that, as is the case with many therapies, the least affected clients could show the most gain. He considers that, when the narrator has been successful in meeting life's problems, a review is a good strategy. His implicit opinion seems to be that, for those who had been unsuccessful at problem solving, the challenge of review would simply become one more hurdle to stumble at. Edinberg (1985) recommends review therapy for clients who have the verbal and cognitive ability both to recall previous events and to achieve some insight into them. He advises that it should be directed at individuals who have had enough positive experiences in life, so that review will not be a depressing experience.

While review is widely practised, it is particularly important for people in crisis, who need support in order to feel more in control of their own lives, face their attitudes to self and others, and work on accepting or changing these as necessary.

Scenario 8

Harry had been a Royal Marine in a family tradition going back to Nelson. A self-effacing individual, he said very little about his service life, although he travelled widely in the British Empire of the 1920s. After five years of this he came home and reported that he wanted to buy himself out. His father was scornful and his mother reminded him that jobs were scarce.

Uncharacteristically, Harry insisted that he would do anything rather than go back. Eventually, he had his way, got a ladder and a bicycle, and 'got on his bike' to work as a window cleaner.

Forty years later, retired and in an advanced stage of the hereditary disease that was to lead to his death within twelve months, Harry shocks the family as they are taking Sunday tea together. Out of the blue, he talks about an episode in Smyrna, where he was part of a detachment guarding the British Consulate. Riots were going on and Turks began to massacre the local people. A woman was beheaded within a few yards of the line of Marines. The men were under orders not to fire: some of them were gripping their rifles so hard that the blood burst from their fingernails. During the night the officer in charge of the detachment left the Consulate and took to the hills to fight for the resistance. 'It was unheard of for a Marine to do that sort of thing,' says Harry, shaking his head, 'unheard of.'

- **What was Harry trying to communicate to his family?**
- **Putting yourself in the place of a family member at the table, how might you have responded?**

(See Chapter 9, p. 150.)

Words are the most common medium for review, but they are not the only way to convey a story. In extreme circumstances, they cannot do enough to convey intense feelings.

In relating his experience as a prisoner of war of the Japanese, and recounting how he felt when his captors taunted him by indicating in sign language that they would eat him, Ted often has to resort to mime in order to convey their predatory movements and threats, and his alternating terror and frozen watchfulness.

Jackie, a widow and a dementia sufferer, communicates with very few words. Conventional social boundaries (who is this person? do I know them well enough to trust them with a secret?) disappear as she conveys to her listener her feelings on the death of her husband by miming the action of slitting her wrists.

The objective of the listener throughout is to pay attention to the voice of narrative. This may be done not only by attending to the meaning of what is said or not said, but also by registering and responding to non-verbal behaviour indicative of feelings accompanying what is being said. The literature does not often explore how the experience of telling a story feels to the narrator, and we shall return to this point in the following chapters.

Non reviewers

The subject of contraindications has attracted only a modest amount of attention in the literature. Lewis and Butler (1974) recognise that some older people prefer to carry out a solo review and would resent a therapist's attention. For Coleman (1988) too, review may sometimes be a private matter, as he finds that people do not necessarily want or benefit from the help of a counsellor in 'putting their house in order'. Verwoerdt (1981), on the other hand, considers that review is intimately related to the notion of what one is and has been for others. A need for forgiveness and reconciliation may be felt, and the most direct way of meeting this would be to involve another. Brink advises against review therapy being used with narrators whose experience has been in general unsuccessful and painful.

Should persons with dementia be excluded? Lewis and Butler view brain damage as not necessarily a contraindication. Woods *et al.* (1992) conclude that review can be conducted with persons with dementia, but it should be noted that the studies they report deal more with general reminiscence activities, which in themselves can yield worthwhile intervals of satisfaction and pleasure for participants, without proceeding to resolution of long-standing problems or the achievement of goals such as integrity.

Gender issues

It has been suggested that early developmental difference relates to women being predominantly the child rearers, which influences the interpersonal dynamics of gender formation. Mothers experience their daughters as continuous with themselves, and attachment fuses with identity. Mothers view boys as opposite; boys' identity becomes aligned to separateness. Girls retain the basis for 'empathy' built into their primary sense of self; boys cannot. Developmental challenges are separating and relationship respectively, according to Chodorow (1978).

Scenario 9

From her review, Louise, 28, appears an exception to these generalisations. Intrigued and puzzled because many elements of her lifestyle seem to be selected on the basis of 'if your mother wouldn't like it, it must be all right', she recalls a succession of memories themed around resistance to her mother.

In the course of life review with Heather, a counsellor, she reports that the earliest of these was of a white wall in her childhood home in Bermuda being covered by scrawls of green paint. Triggered by 'a row, with her, over something I can't remember', as a toddler she was 'getting even'. Unsatisfied with the effect of the paint, she then found cups and saucers from the best teaset, broke them, and set about blocking the drains with the pieces. A recital of other events follows, leading up to a present in which she finds herself taking drugs she doesn't enjoy and living with a man she despises – 'all because she would have hated it – we've lost touch now, but I know she would have'. Louise becomes silent and preoccupied.

- **In Heather's place, how might you have dealt with Louise's silence?**
- **How would you have proceeded to work with Louise?**

(See Chapter 9, p. 151.)

For Tannen (1987), while communication is always a matter of balancing conflicting needs for involvement and independence, women often have a relatively greater need for involvement, and men a relatively greater need for independence. Being understood without saying what you mean gives a pay-off in involvement, and that is why women value it so highly, she suggests. Tannen advises that, if you want to be understood without saying what you mean explicitly in words, you must convey meaning somewhere else – in how words are spoken, or by meta-messages (communications about relationships between people). Women are often more attuned than men to the meta-messages of talk. When women surmise meaning in this way, it seems mysterious to men, who call it 'women's intuition' (if they think it's right), or 'reading things in' (if they think it's wrong), Tannen comments wryly.

Scenario 10

Meta-messages often occur in life review and can indeed be difficult to decode. Gillian, a depressed middle-aged mother, is complaining that her unworthiness was made apparent by the fact that her 30-year-old only son who lives in the United States had not written to her for three months.

She had not written in that time because she was waiting for his reply to her previous letter. Asked how that letter had concluded, she recalls her postscript, 'don't come to my funeral'. The listener, Brian, a community nurse, suggests that possibly the son might have misunderstood her message. Gillian is shocked at this idea. The real message had been quite clear, she protests. There was no possibility that her communication could have been misunderstood.

- **What made Brian suggest that the postscript could have been misunderstood?**
- **What ideas do you have about what 'the real message' could have been?**

(See Chapter 9, p. 152.)

Separate moral development paths for men and women are a critical line of psychological development in the lives of both sexes. Women's moral development, rooted in the intimacy and importance of relationship and care, is traditionally ascribed to men much later on in their developmental trajectories, Gilligan (1982) has suggested. Study of women's experience highlights that moral problems arise from conflicting responsibilities rather than competing rights. Resolution comes through contextual thinking around the understanding of relative responsibilities, rather than a more formal abstract approach to understanding rights and rules.

The substance of women's moral concern lies in attending to voices different from their own, and to others' judgements as well as their own. This concern for relationship is easily misconstrued in models of development that focus on individual achievement. It is more likely to be perceived as 'weakness' and confusion of judgement, rather than relational strength. Sometimes family issues are difficult to unravel. But it is not uncommon to be able to get to the heart of the matter by pinning down one or two key incidents or statements that had a disproportionate impact and which need to be re-examined.

Scenario 11

Cecily, an 81-year-old widow, lives alone. She suffers from recurrent depression, and often speaks of killing herself because she does not deserve to live. Her life is 'useless to anyone, without meaning'. She sees herself as inadequate, and 'just not good enough'. More than that, it was actually dangerous to allow herself to get too close to others. Wondering aloud how it came about that Cecily had come to think of herself in this way, Vicky, a social worker, encourages Cecily to explore her life history.

For several weeks nothing unusual emerges. Then she remembers an incident when she was 10. An only child who was big for her age and a tomboy, uncomfortable in a dress, she fought at school, protecting younger children against bullies. She came back one day with dirt on her clothes, a bruised knee, and a grazed face. Her mother preparing tea in the farmhouse kitchen threw up her hands in horror: 'Cecily! You'll never come to any good!'

- **As Vicky, how might you explore this memory with Cecily?**
- **How would you examine ways of challenging its continuing relevance for her and its implications for her sense of self?**

(See Chapter 9, p. 152.)

The Western social construction of gender applauds men who develop wisdom via increased sensitivity as they age. Older and wiser women do not enact their maturity differently from men; but in the social and cultural construction of wisdom in a particular culture they may be seen differently. The archetypal older person is seen as being characterised by losses in old age, and responses and reactions to losses. There is scope for wise acceptance, stimulation of late creativity, and fury at frustration of still-remaining potentials. This is the healthy side of energetic assertions frequently shown in late life (Hubback, 1996).

Mourners

Molinari and Reichlin (1984–5) see life review in terms of mourning, with stages encompassing: reorganisation of relationship to the lost other; obsessive recounting and reiteration; reflection on self-absorption; and the end result, learning to relinquish what has been lost. Such business-like phrases hardly do justice to the frenetic struggle of the narrator who is 'hanging on like grim death' to a lost other.

Scenario 12

Alan, a social worker, is visiting Jacintha, 58, because she is not caring for herself, and her concerned family and neighbours do not know what to do. Alan discovers that Jacintha was widowed two years before in particularly distressing circumstances. Her devoted husband who would have done anything for her stepped out of line for once by going for a walk by himself against her wishes. She was unwell and had hoped that he would have stayed to keep her company. He should have realised this. On the walk, within a few minutes of their home, a bus knocked him down. He died in hospital.

She had reacted with extreme and enduring guilt, but initially would not directly confront her anger at her husband for having gone against her wishes and having had the last word as he left the house. Red-faced and with veins standing out on her forehead, she claims: 'I blame the bus company. I blame the surgeons. I blame God. But angry with him? Me?'

- **As Alan, how would you respond?**
- **Would life review be useful for Jacintha?**

(See Chapter 9, p. 153.)

Eastern and Western views of knowing oneself diverge (Nitis, 1989). The scenarios quoted so far are from a Western viewpoint – from

European, American, or Australian contexts – because our experience and study have been in these settings. Review happens elsewhere in ways not dissimilar to Western practice: for example, in Morita therapy in Japan depressed patients are required to spend one hour a day writing about their feelings. Sometimes, as in the following example, divergence is more striking.

Scenario 13
Michiko, a Japanese woman in her sixties, seeks advice from the monk who is administrator of the Zen retreat where she is a housekeeper. She reports having been told by her doctor that she has incurable cancer and will die soon. Since she has heard this, she has become very frightened. Partly it is the fear of dying, but partly also doubt. She has spent years in Zen training with a Master at the retreat and she feels that a person who has been deeply immersed in, and derived something from, Zen training should be able to die serenely.

She is troubled that if she were to die in an undignified, tortured way, this would be shameful for herself, and reflect badly on the teacher whom she had admired so much. However much she tries to escape, this worry remains with her day and night. So she has come to ask about it. 'I have practised to my utmost but I still have doubt about death. Where was the mistake in my practice – where has it gone wrong that I should still feel this? If my practice had really borne fruit, surely now I should be able to face death with more equanimity and peace.'

- **How would you respond?**

(See Chapter 9, p. 154.)

Sometimes a story has to be recounted by proxy, through an intermediary. This was the case with Susan, a 'difficult and demanding' new resident in a residential home.

Scenario 14
Susan often seeks to go home in the middle of the night. Her protests at these times seem to relate to experiences much earlier in her life, and staff report that she appears to regress to childhood. Susan is unwilling and possibly unable to talk about her childhood, but she agrees with Terry, the psychologist at the nursing home, that her son Bob can give an account on her behalf.

'Mum's mother died when mum was just a very young child. Mum often told us of how they were very poor. One of the neighbours used to take pity on them and give them something to eat. When I say they were very poor mum had four sisters and two brothers. From what I can gather her dad was quite good to them except when he had been out drinking. She told me that when he came back home they would run and hide in case he took his anger out on them. When my mum was still young her dad married again and started another family. Mum was put into an orphanage. I think she was there until she was old enough to work. When she started work it was mainly in service . . .

'To sum up, mum was and still is a lovely mum, very loving although she never showed it with kisses and hugs (as she does since she had a stroke). She always worried about us, would do anything for us. She would have given us her last penny. I suspect mum was not used to being hugged and kissed as a child and that she was quite sad and lonely. In fact she said she was lonely. I think perhaps, from what mum has said, the orphanage was quite strict and there was (sic) quite a few rules. I think mum sometimes thinks she is in an orphanage now, and that is why she keeps asking what shall I do now, please help me. I think mum is also very frustrated by not being able to do things for herself.'

- **As Terry, would you use this information to work with Susan and her carers?**
- **If so, what would you do?**

(See Chapter 9, p. 155.)

Some narrators are primarily concerned to present an apology for their life and to 'explain' the origin of their current untoward behaviour. The following extracts are from a document prepared by Mandy, a 59-year-old widow, for review work. (Her spelling and grammar have not been corrected.) She had a history of multiple ineffectual contacts with myriad health and social care agencies, and had told her latest contact that she wanted to find out: 'Why I keep coming to see people like you.'

Sort of thing just to make you feel nearly a criminal. I have to do my sentence like a zombie, I was called a Model prisoner I was liked very much I was afraid most of the time. I used to sleep my time away you get some very bad people dangerous there three kinds the real criminals the stupid and the down and outs that need a home when the morning comes the smell of the slop buckets one woman watches the other try to start a Rowe

It was in 1966 year that my trouble started. It was for fraud from littlewoods mail order I was Sentenced to 1 year in prison my first offence which was harsh, then in 1969 I got another sentence of 2 years some thing which was a terrible Experience

Transferred to open prison, the I escaped got caught had to spend 2 weeks in Solitary Cell then sent back to another prison my Life was hell then I went to Holloway but the horrors I saw mixed with Murders – MYRA HINDLEY lesbeons but I was liked. I got through it but like a zombie, then in 1972 I got another had police round the Door 4 times a day could never be in the house but they did not get me I moved away . . .

A review in a family can sometimes take on the tone of a séance, with the internalised voice of an authority figure from the family's history breaking in and sounding loud and clear over the years.

Scenario 15
Len, a 59-year-old retired pharmacist, lives with his wife Rose, a former teacher. Approaching his retirement, four years before, they had a bungalow built for them, but the construction was faulty, the builder could not or would not correct it, and Len became very depressed. He told Rose they should kill themselves – this was 'the only way out of this mess'.

With psychiatric treatment, the depression lifted and Len had a trouble-free three years. He then began to be withdrawn and preoccupied with his bowel functioning, claiming that he would become chronically constipated and die from accumulated toxins. Sally, his family doctor, asks Len what evidence he has for this belief, and where it came from. After some discussion, he acknowledges that his mother thought her children should start each day by opening their bowels. A 'dose of the jollop' (laxative) would be administered each day and, before they left for school, she would ask (here Len's voice is strikingly different from his usual monotone): 'Have you been?'

Rose is shocked. 'Len, that's your mother speaking. That's her voice!'

- **In Sally's place, how would you respond?**

(See Chapter 9, p. 156.)

Review is not only for individuals. In systemic approaches, couples and family groups are increasingly involved in reflection on their history – how they were formed and maintained, and how they can be sustained; and on how rules were shaped and procedures learned. The 'family shield' exercise favoured by some family therapists is a case in point. The family is asked to construct a coat of arms and a motto or mottoes depicting how the family presents itself to its members and to the world in general. Assumptions about what is to be expected grow over several generations. They may need to be explored retrospectively before the family can move forward.

For example, adult caregivers of an ageing parent can face a crisis of filial maturity, recognising that they have to take over some aspects of 'parental' responsibility for their parent. Such crisis may tap a need for review, with the objectives of decreasing anxiety in all concerned, and attainment of a developmental period characterised by filial maturity (Murray *et al.*, 1995). Family balance can be thrown into turmoil as authority is transferred from one generation to another. The following example is from Garland and Garland, 1995.

Scenario 16

Dave and his wife Glenys are carers for Don, Dave's father. Don suffers from a dementing illness but is still able to cope after a fashion in his own house. Dave and Glenys live only ten minutes away, and one or other looks in two or three times a day, including last thing 'to see him all right for the night', to check on the old man's well-being.

He is increasingly forgetful, and Gloria, a caseworker from a family support agency, is supporting the couple who are particularly worried about his safety and security. Dave feels torn between his responsibility to his wife and their children and his responsibility to his father. He gets especially angry with Don for calling him 'Dad', and at a family meeting where this happens repeatedly he accuses Don: 'Stop winding me up. I'm not your dad – you're my dad! OK?' The old man smiles and nods obediently: 'OK, Dad.'

Before Dave could explode yet again, Gloria intervenes to ask Glenys and Dave a question reviewing his recent experience with Don.

- **What was Gloria's question?**
- **What was she trying to establish?**

(See Chapter 9, p. 156.)

In striving to make sense of life stories, the experienced listener needs to tap wisdom-related criteria (without becoming self-satisfied and feeling like the fount of all wisdom). Review may be understood as an avenue to access wisdom-related knowledge. Theorists and practitioners need to bear in mind the criteria for wisdom-related review judgements identified by Staudinger *et al.* (1992): factual and procedural knowledge about life, life span contextualism, relativism of values, recognition, and management of uncertainty.

- **Thinking point**
  How would you be true to yourself as narrator of your life story?

Chapter 6, 'Review in sequence', introduces guidelines for practice.

Chapter 6

Review in sequence

SUMMARY A would-be listener should prepare with a personal review. Review has three modes: unstructured; semi-structured; or relatively structured in the context of counselling or therapy. A cycle of preparation, opening, maintaining, closing, and following up is described. Review exercises are discussed with examples.

Readers will already be engaging in review from time to time. It is natural for an individual to be psychologically minded, and to experiment to see how far it is possible to get by on one's own efforts rather than to seek to 'do it by the book'. Before beginning with volunteer subjects or with clients, it is to be expected that would-be listeners resemble them in having a history of attempts at review that will have been developed sporadically, in varying ways and with fluctuating levels of commitment and consistency. Because of this it is advisable to know oneself by narrating one's own story clearly and fully before venturing into reviewing others' lives. Without doing so it is difficult to appreciate the obstacles that can emerge in the process, and to understand how to negotiate them.

In this chapter grounding is given on how to prepare review, as listener, and as narrator, and how to open, maintain, close, and follow-up a cycle of activity. The authors offer training exercises, and illustrate these with their own responses. A continuing process of exposure to engaging in review and learning with support and supervision will be necessary to test and practise the ideas and methods set out below.

Three modes

The review modes described overlap: for example, 1 continues while 2 or 3 are going on (a factor that listeners in 2 or 3 do well to remember). Some of the differences between 1 and 3 relate to the distinction between sympathy as in befriending, and empathy as in counselling or therapy.

Mode 1 includes self-generated review by individuals, couples, or families. Much of this may be internal reflection, spontaneous and unplanned. Friends may be involved as listeners; and volunteers, community workers, care staff, family doctors, or priests may also be drawn in. Often such review is on a one-off or 'as required' basis, and it may be more likely to occur on significant occasions such as anniversaries, ceremonies, reunions, and other get-togethers. It can also take place over a considerable interval of time if a protracted issue such as educational or career planning, moving home, adjustment to new surroundings, or ups and downs in the process of growing up, is being dealt with.

In this mode relatively brief informal contacts are the norm. Privacy, while helpful, is not always considered essential. The narrator takes issues as they arise, displaying parts of a life, as though moving around a mirror to pick out an angle for inspection. In general the narrator is already engaged and may or may not be willing to share this process with a listener. This mode may be done anywhere, at any time. If there are sufficient reasons to do so, the narrator-listener may proceed to Mode 2 or 3, but moving on is an option that many narrators choose not to take, even when the listener or listeners may press them because the emerging story appears to merit closer attention.

Mode 2 is characteristic of reminiscence groups in residential and community settings. It includes groups for guided autobiography (Birren and Birren, 1995) and journal workshops (Progoff, 1975), and the review programmes outlined by contributors to Haight and Webster (1995), and usually has a timetable of sessions. Listeners have some training, support, and supervision, and a degree of structure and direction is offered to narrators, many of whom are volunteers. Contacts tend to be sustained and planned with time set aside; they are more structured and longer; and issues of privacy and confidentiality are considered with more care.

The listener works through an agenda with each narrator, exploring predetermined segments of the stories under review. The narrator is not necessarily engaged in review when this mode is started up, and may need encouragement to start, and have mixed reactions to the experience of having a listener, or may take some time to come to terms with being in a group where others' stories are heard. What is being offered is not always clear: activity, community project, education, intervention, oral history – a number of terms are used for what goes on in this mode. What is not on offer is counselling or therapy: the listener needs to refer on, with the agreement of the narrator concerned, if therapy appears to be required.

Mode 3 is review in the context of counselling and therapy; it is relatively more structured by a contract between listener and narrator. Particular issues of adjustment are being confronted. The review is usually a component of what is being offered, as it is rare to find counselling or therapy being identified solely with reviewing a client's life. Its relative importance in the package varies according to the theoretical persuasion of the professional listener or listeners.

They and the narrator or narrators are expected to establish commitment to working together with a specified agenda and goals. The narrator has come, willingly or unwillingly, to a professional because they or others feel some life issues need to resolved. It may not be clear what these are, but it appears that something is wrong or missing, and well-being is reduced. Often the narrator is actively engaged in a personal review before referral, and wants to speed up, to take the process deeper. Review in Modes 1 or 2 may have been attempted only to become blocked or derailed, or review in these modes may have been evaded or deferred, and the narrator may have been overtaken by crisis. This chapter deals primarily with practice in Modes 1 and 2, and the following chapter takes up the cycle in Mode 3. As these modes have similar concerns in many respects a number of the points made here also apply to Mode 3, and the cycle is the same.

Preparation

Published guidelines are not easy to find. From the limited literature and our experience we recommend the following.

Put yourself in the narrator's place

With a colleague, share a personal review within a framework modelled on co-counselling. Guidelines for topics to be dealt with are offered by interview protocols such as those described in Kimmel (1990) and Haight and Webster (see Appendix). While many interview schedules take an orderly chronological approach, working from child through to adult, be prepared to consider, if you and the narrator have the latitude, starting with the present and working backwards, as this helps the narrator to appreciate review's continuing relevance for the present.

Select an approach

Many have been used: Progoff recommends individual journal-keeping to a prescribed format; Gersie and King (1990) describe use of group story-making exercises to further individuation; Viney (1993) draws on a personal construct perspective to analyse life-story themes invoked by older adults; and Birren and Birren describe courses with a model of further education for seniors. Family or close friends may be involved in a review to explore a range of viewpoints, either throughout or at a particular stage when relationships come to the fore.

Systems as well as individuals have life stories that need a close look from time to time. Away-days, seminars with independent facilitators, sensitivity training groups, and many other formats are used by an increasing number of organisations to this end. Informal systems such as families or friendship groups tend to depend on improvisation for their review needs. In cases where there is little interest in or opportunity for contact between all key members at one time, systems can become dysfunctional, in part, at least, because there is no shared story path for members to follow.

- **Thinking point**
  Choose a system in which you are involved. How would you set up and run a review session for its members?

Consider a culture and its resources

In a residential or community care setting, attention needs to be given to developing a culture in which review is encouraged. Group story-making exercises can make a positive contribution in providing a climate in which narrators feel supported in transcending pressures to 'keep yourself to yourself'. Potential narrators need to be able to ask themselves why they might like to review, and to explore parallels with television programmes such as *This is Your Life*. With agreement, they can examine someone else's recorded life to see how it's done, listen to life stories on tape or watch filmed interviews, participate in designing the format of their prospective review (see below), and participate in consulting friends and family to join the process.

Give special attention to discussing with the narrator the rationale for the proposed intervention, and its scope. Get a clear view of what is happening. Resources to be assembled can include a tape recorder or dictaphone – for the narrator to use, if possible, to retain control of the proceedings – a still camera and film, or a video camera. Consent forms may be required. The format of any written record can be planned with the narrator, including layout, typeface, colours, and other presentation. A fold-out book with back-to-back display is preferable to a scrapbook. An organiser of review needs to make clear who pays for what, to avoid embarrassment.

Identify sources of information

These may include: narrator; relatives, friends, and other carers; albums of photos and other memorabilia; existing family tapes; greeting cards; certificates; cuttings; notes, records, videos of outings, shows, parties (if institutional); community team access; old medical records; local authority notes; local library and museum resources. Visits could be made to significant places, including birthplace, homes, school, church, family graves. Some visits may be part of future plans. A companion and perhaps transport, if required, will need to be arranged.

Practise listening skills

There are many introductory texts on the general topic of learning how to listen (for example, Egan, 1998), and those engaging in review would be well advised to become grounded in at least one generic training in how to listen. It is essential to be an attentive listener and to be able to keep up a conversational framework, using open-ended questions – 'How does that make you feel?' 'Tell me more about this' – and being prepared to respond to emotions: 'Remembering this makes you feel . . .', 'You look as though you're feeling . . .'.

Like Sherlock Holmes the master detective, the listener must be alert to the dog that doesn't bark in the night, aware that what doesn't happen can be a clue to what has happened. This can be the case with a narrator's omissions or distortions, such as talking about one parent but never mentioning the other, or idealising (Edinberg, 1985, talks of 'glorifying') a spouse or child. It must be recognised that, in the interest of the narrator's need to reduce cognitive dissonance, fact and fantasy can mingle in review.

It is necessary to cultivate ability to stay with potentially painful topics where appropriate in a constructive way, and in parallel with this also the ability to disengage where appropriate, given the intense and personal nature of review. Narrators can be cued beforehand that they have the right to choose their topics, and to seek a break or a change of subject if they want. Listeners retain the responsibility of choosing not to engage if they do not wish to or do not feel competent to listen; and to disengage if the review enters areas that they do not feel to be appropriate.

Define expectations

Prepare yourself and the narrator with care. Agree boundaries. There are different expectations for the conversation that is to take place within each review mode. Review the rationale for the process (see 'Why review?' Chapter 2, p. 28). If you are working intensively it is particularly important (unless you are listening to Scheherazade and have a thousand and one nights to spare!) to agree a limit to the number of sessions. Be exact in contracting with the client what each of you is going to undertake. Arrange supervision where appropriate.

Select narrators

Narrators with a severe intellectual impairment, those who are severely depressed, and those who are preoccupied with their physical state tend to see review as irrelevant and unrewarding even if they can be persuaded to engage. Target storytellers who spontaneously have already begun to review but have become stuck (usually this is because, like most forms of working on the self, unusual self-discipline is required and they do not feel equal to their self-imposed task). The best way of finding out whether a person is in review is simply to ask. Remember, though, that it is not always simple for the respondent to answer. Review sometimes takes place in an oblique fashion, sidling up to the narrator from time to time, briefly emerging on the threshold of consciousness, and fading again, like a half-remembered item on a shopping list that has been left at home. In such cases, if the narrator agrees, it may be necessary to search for clues that reminiscence is in fact stirring. For instance, reports of being troubled by disquieting dreams, in which the past is being repeatedly revisited as old exams are resat or old haunts re-explored, sometimes are a pointer.

Set structure

Both focused questioning and free-range discussion are necessary in review. The listener should recognise that reminders, interruptions, and prompts will be needed from both sides, and even that the roles of listener and narrator may be interchangeable. There is a mediation role too, which either may need to step in to at short notice if serious disagreement occurs. Use a framework of questions after considering what questions the listener would wish to ask in the course of the review, and the narrator would accept as appropriate.

Any structure needs to be a frame rather than a cage, and in the course of review you and the narrator may well move outside this list to invent new and productive questions. Taping sessions by agreement frees you both to pay attention to what is being communicated. Both of you can learn a lot from what is going on through tapes and/or transcripts, between sessions. The listener may need to be flexible in the order in which topics are dealt with. If listener or narrator come up with new questions, so much the better.

Choosing words

Phrases or words favoured by the narrator should be taken up and used by the listener to describe what is happening. This is not only to show that the listener is in fact listening, but more fundamentally because favoured turns of phrase or metaphors are themselves ways in to a closer contact with a narrator's experience. For example, 'When you came in, you told me you felt "panned out". Help me understand a bit more how that feels'; or 'As you said a little while ago, perhaps we'll have to cross that bridge when we come to it. I'm wondering, when you are coming up to this kind of bridge what happens to make you decide whether to go on or turn back?'

Maintaining the process

Supervision will be needed, particularly by the inexperienced listener who needs to be helped to realise the importance of time as a resource, the mechanics of getting notes transcribed and processed, and to think in advance about commitment. Help may be needed with respect for confidentiality, with the listener raising the issue to remind those narrators who are so pleased to find someone to listen to their story that they should think through the implications of sharing personal feelings with another. Supervision can also cover such issues as how to gain access to official information – records, medical or nursing notes – bearing in mind service policies on the use of information.

Consulting the narrator about any recording equipment to be used, checking this, and encouraging the client to use it where appropriate are important. Remember that the narrator may know much more than you think about their life (even if they have communication difficulties). Help the narrator's efforts to make sense and see connections. Be attentive to their characteristic views and ways of coping. Remember that the narrator may repeat the same story several times with variations that may need to be reflected and cleared up. Suggest rather than directly contradict. Ask if there might be another explanation, rather than accuse the narrator of getting facts wrong. Remember that careful judgement is required about using third-party information. Be sensitive to gender differences: men may be more likely to tell stories in a linear, chronological way, and attempt to stay more in control; while women may tend to spotlight particular events, and focus on significant objects.

Compiling the story

Use first person throughout to make ownership of the story clear and to increase its feeling of immediacy. This is more congenial for most narrators, who appreciate your interest in the person they are now, and it encourages them to make links with present experience. Support the narrator in using memory prompts if needed. Check whether any misunderstandings have crept in and monitor the accuracy of your recording, session by session. Be prepared to stop at any time if the narrator asks. If you're using a written record, use a distinct colour or typeface, or use italic, to indicate where comments are the listener's rather than the narrator's. Involve the narrator in any editing procedures and invite them to choose the title of the final version of their story. Be sparing in use of subheadings. Make acknowledgements of assistance. Include a section relating to the future, with an action plan. Provide spare sheets for continuation of the review if the narrator should wish.

Consider self-disclosure

In moderation, self-disclosure by the listener not only directly models the behaviour requested of the volunteer or client, but also indirectly helps them to take the role of their problem-solver. Intuitively, it can be more attractive for them to begin with 'if I were you' before turning to 'if I were me'.

Here, the authors compare notes to illustrate this.

Christina: *I think everyone tells stories about themselves. I tell one: about belly-dancing in a Cairo night club. We went there with some Arabs but were whisked off by another group who took us to another club and plied us with Black Label whisky. I remember being impressed because one of the men was a singer in the club. He dedicated a song to me and asked me to dance on stage. In my mind it is like a scene from a movie. I was quite drunk and I'm convinced they also spiked our drinks because I remember feeling quite detached from reality, almost like having an out of body experience. I also felt it was all very wild and decadent and quite romantic. It says something about me wanting to be seen as provocative and a rebel.*

I don't know about sharing this with a client! It is interesting how you present yourself to others in terms of the memories you select. Those memories that you choose to share say a lot about how you would like to be seen as well as how you see yourself. The story could be used in a counselling session if the client had difficulty with storytelling. I might share my memory of dancing (without the details!) with them. Then I would ask them if they have a story they tell people when they first meet and what they think that says about them.

Jeff: *It depends on the client's needs, too. I sometimes meet a narrator who is still consumed with regret about something they did or did not do as a child, and they are still saying 'if only . . .'*

In such a case we could look at the possibility of reframing their perception. This might be on the lines of: 'Yes, this happened. I took what seemed to be a feasible line at the time, within the limits of my capacity and understanding. It's finished with now unless I choose to go on digging it up. Perhaps I can run it by just one more time, learn something useful from what happened, and apply it to my present and future.' If there is some difficulty in this process, so that the narrator does not appear to understand this approach or reacts with 'it's all very well for you . . .', and we had an established relationship, I might tell them a story. Perhaps this one:

I can remember myself at 8 years old waking up late at night to hear my parents having a row downstairs in the kitchen. I sat on the stairs listening, hearing roaring and snarling (I know you can't hear snarling, but that's what I thought of). My reaction was: 'Just like animals.' The thought crossed my mind that I should intervene, but it didn't sound safe.

I felt scared and so went back to bed and tried to shut out the noise. I decided in future to keep quiet and stay out of the way, not just with them but also outside. If it's like this at home, what's it like out there?

At this point I would turn to the narrator, explain that over time I had reframed this episode within my story, and ask them to speculate about how this had been done. When we had completed that, and having thanked them, I would then invite them to share an episode, so we could apply what we had learned together to their contribution.

Exercises

Exercises such as 'first memory' (p. 111), 'lifeline' (p. 112), or 'decisions' (p. 113), not only improve the listener's subjective understanding of review, but can also be used by the narrator during review and/or between sessions, to get both away from the feeling that they are caught up in a question and answer interrogation.

Taping

If sessions are taped, with the narrator's agreement, this can free you both to pay attention to how the narrator is communicating through body language. Also, both of you can learn a lot about what is going on by studying the tapes between sessions and returning at the following session to moments that either of you have considered significant.

Respect

Show emphatic and empathic respect for the narrator's life story. Many storytellers are unduly self-effacing and need to have their achievements recognised and underlined so that they stand out. Lifetime achievement awards are presented to entertainers who have made their mark in a career. Medals – such as the Purple Heart for the US military – are awarded for being wounded in combat. Each life review can be celebrated in its own way as it marks success – if only in survival, and progress in learning – even if much remains to be learned.

Reframe if necessary

A narrator may be given to self-deprecation over past 'sins' of commission or omission. Sometimes it is necessary to encourage a different, more positive perspective. Explore the probability that, using the information and other resources that appeared available to them at the time, they made the best choice that could have been made.

When reviewers look back they often begin with 'if only', berating themselves for having been 'stupid' or 'weak'. It is necessary to persist with encouragement to reframe, separating actor from act. Hindsight always has 20/20 vision; and the important issue now is to recognise that they have come through adversity, rather than to stay with the question of how that adversity arose. In such a situation we prefer to encourage the narrator to come to the point of putting the realisation in their own words, which will mean more to them than ours.

Remember the present

Return to the present at intervals. Encourage use of the present tense as far as possible, particularly when the narrator is exploring vivid episodes from the past that they acknowledge are still affecting present thoughts and feelings. This tends to bring a greater sense of immediacy even when dealing with 'past' events; it fosters closer involvement with the experience being described; and it underlines the belief that the past is still alive in the present and open to review.

Cue the narrator with 'let's get back to now', or a similar phrase, if they are dwelling on the past at undue length. The listener will know when this point comes – each of us has a variety of subjective signals from our previous experience of conversations that have gone off course, leaving us adrift and floundering.

We should be able to recognise the Ancient Mariner syndrome as it arises. (The eponymous narrator in Coleridge's poem waylaid a guest en route to a wedding and showed no compunction in launching into his harrowing monologue. The wedding guest beat his breast in frustration, but to no avail.) The listener needs to be ready with a range of reminders, interruptions, and prompts that will be more effective than breast-beating.

Introduce progress

It may be necessary to explore scope for a new story line, while seeking to discover how the narrator's current coping strategies have been shaped by the events they relate. For example, the listener may comment: 'Your mother told you this when you were 6. You are now 26. Who is deciding you should still listen to her? You are? What might you do about that?' Explore their perception of the room they have now to develop alternative strategies, while recognising (Smail, 1996) the reality of the social constraints on the individual's ability to make major psychological changes.

Feelings

Even 'bad' feelings need not only to be accepted but also to be encouraged. For example, the listener may need to be prepared to mirror the narrator's change of expression, intake of breath, catching of the voice, finger tapping, head scratching, or fist clenching, which signals arousal, and encourage the narrator to be aware of what is happening within them at that moment and to express it in words. This must be done with care and used with discretion in Modes 1 and 2 if the narrator is not to feel uncomfortably exposed by such intervention. It is best to limit this to those moments in the narration when the story has reached a crisis point but appears to be blocked, or when the story being told is clearly discrepant from the narrator's accompanying behaviour.

Bringing review to life

It can be helpful to amplify the narrator's presentation by prompting them to use a variety of reference points to define their life. One might say: 'If it were a book, what kind of a book would it be?' Each of us can be viewed as a story or stories within a book, and this idea is popularly expressed in such sayings as 'I could read him like a book' or 'you can't judge a book by its cover'. Alternatively, a film, a party, a room, a painting, a pub, a dance, or a journey might be used – the possibilities are unlimited. The key principles are to use whatever chimes in with the storyteller's background, lifestyle, or ambitions; and to recognise that a number of categories might be needed to get the full flavour. Within some of these categories several exemplars might be employed to tap aspects that change over time.

Family and friends

Others may be involved directly in review, if the narrator wishes and with their agreement, to add a helpful perspective on the topic. Truth is relative in any story, and other perspectives can add the all-important social dimension to review and provide cross-referencing.

Review aims to identify the narrator's truth as far as possible, but where family and friends are closely involved there are multiple truths and the best that may be achieved is a degree of consensus that often is fragile.

Pick up 'Waving and Drowning' signals

We use this term for indications by the narrator that they are in an uncomfortable and possibly dangerous position and are indicating this by using expressions such as, 'I need to pick myself up' . . . 'I'm pulled both ways' . . . 'We're coming to the crunch.' Encourage the narrator to enact and re-enact how getting into such contorted positions actually feels, what consequences it has, and what the options are for taking up a stance with which they and others in their life would feel more secure.

Possessions

These can be used as triggers for review. For example, in a reminiscence group a man produced a 'never absent, never late' medal he had been awarded for Sunday School attendance. He then explained that it should have been given to his sister, as she had been the driving force behind his attendance each week. With the lively assistance of women in the group he was encouraged to reflect that this pattern continued into the present – his wife drove him to the group and picked him up, and she had persuaded him to attend in the first place.

Varying media

Vary the media used. A Desert Island Discs or karaoke session could be appropriate for the musically inclined, with encouragement to select music of particular significance for them. Favourite poems can be read and their associations explored (Magee, 1988b). A life history painting or series of sketches could be 'commissioned' from a narrator interested in art. A photo album could be scanned, an attic explored, or a house extended over the years could be toured. Such approaches are particularly suitable for narrators who are focused on doing rather than discussing, but who often come to life when they are moving over territory that feels secure and familiar to them.

Dreaming

Some narrators will report dreaming more than usual (Magee, 1991a), just before, during, and immediately after they engage in review. They should be encouraged to expect that this could happen, and to keep a bedside notebook for immediate recording of content, as this can provide interesting reflection on the parallel process of review.

Closing

To establish continuity, bridging tasks should be given between sessions, encouraging the narrator to think through the next set of topics in advance. This could include inviting them to set up an agenda for the following session, to highlight a particular theme for special attention, or to identify a topic that they have determined not to deal with and reflect on why this decision has been reached. Most sessions gain from a summing-up ten minutes before the end. This should be a shared exercise, noting where there is agreement and where there is divergence, and not straining for consensus at any price. As review is ongoing between sessions, the narrator should be encouraged to reflect in a systematic way between sessions. Each summary should include targets for focused reflection to be taken up next time.

The penultimate session should include a presentation by the listener of their understanding of the story so far, accompanied by feedback from the narrator. The last half of the penultimate session should be devoted to winding up, formulating the basis for a summary of the review's findings to be shared in the final session. This may be a written account, an audio- or videotape, or a graphic illustration, or even in multi-media format. The final session focuses on celebration as the narrator accepts the definitive (for now) record, and the listener thanks them. Evaluation at the final session should focus on the perceived usefulness of this record, and its anticipated consequences for reframing and action undertaken or projected.

Follow-up

At around three months follow-up with re-evaluation is advised. Review is a continuing project. The participants need to look at how any action plan is working. If requested by the narrator, the possibility of further sessions should be considered.

Exercises

To aid your learning about review these exercises are intended to draw out your own experience to equip you as a listener. Try them for yourself.

- **Exercise 1**
  Use your mind's eye to recapture your first clear memory or set of memories (this could be of an incident related to you rather than directly remembered by you). Concentrate not only on what you perceive and do, but also on how you are interpreting what is happening, and how you are feeling. Describe this using the present tense. (It is not essential that you should be confident that what you describe happened exactly as you tell it, or even that it happened at all.) Finally, ask yourself how it came about that you are offering this memory: what does it say about the kind of person you are today?

Christina: *This is interesting because even the choosing says something.*

I'm about 6 or 7 and in the classroom at school. I'm standing in front of an easel which has a large piece of paper fastened by a bulldog clip. The paper is covered with daubs of the brightest yellow, blue, green. It is a house with smoke coming from the chimney. I am wearing a white plastic apron. The classroom has windows along one side. It is very satisfying to mix colours in a palette which has the dried residue of previous weeks. I am happy. I also like squeezing paint out, it makes a satisfying noise. I can smell the paint. It feels like I'm almost part of the picture and I think there's a thinner line between fantasy and reality when you're 6 or 7. I feel happy because I'm doing something I like doing and am good at. I think I'm aware of others only on the edges of my vision so others are concentrating as hard as I am. It feels like I'm doing something just for me and no one else. It feels like time is standing still and the only thing that matters is the painting.

I can relate to it now by thinking of the times when I just drift off inside my head during the day. Also when I'm doing something which puts me in touch with nature, like gardening. This has an association with doing the painting as both are primitive and about touching and feeling things. When I work in the garden I seem to see and smell clearly and more vividly too. I think it's important to stop and really look at your surroundings. There are times when it is good just to stop. It reminds me by thinking of this memory how important it is to be creative and find something to do which is absorbing.

Jeff: *Yes. Back in the Sixties, before you were thought of, they called that being 'grounded' or 'being in the here and now'. More recently, Lucinda Williams has a beautiful song about it, 'Side of the Road'. In my first memory:*

I'm about 3 and am walking out in the back garden, having left the house behind me with a feeling of escape. I don't quite know what to do with my freedom and I am aware that my mother's back there in the house keeping an eye on me perhaps. Everything is bright in the sunshine and exceptionally clear: it is as though every blade of grass and every jewel of dew on every blade is visible all at once. I'm startled to hear my name being called, and I look round to next door where my uncle lives with his family. His wife May is calling me and as I go over I see her arm is waving through the trellis that separates the gardens what must be a bundle of comics. Her son used to read them first and then they were passed on to me. I am struck by the darkness of the shadows on the trellis – they are blue-black and intense – and the whiteness of her arm and the sinuous way it moves, like a swan's neck. I'm fascinated – so much that I don't even recall whether I got the comics in the end!

How does this connect with now? When I read Huxley's 'The Doors of Perception' about his experiences on LSD, I realised I'd been tripping then but without the added chemicals. I still get these peak experiences sometimes when the present moment is lit from within. An inner reality, totally secure and ecstatic. It reminds me of how often I get into a reverie where I get lost in wonderment and then get surprised when outer reality breaks in. In a lighter way I remember how I loved comics (words and pictures) and still do. I would read the cornflake packet at breakfast if there was nothing else. And the dark-haired women with pale skin – reader, I married one. The finding of the object is indeed a re-finding.

Christina: *Thank you, professor.*

- **Exercise 2**
  This underlines the personal relevance of life review.
  Reflect on the direction your life has taken to date and on your expectations for the future. Draw your lifeline, from beginning to

anticipated end, with key events, captions, illustrations. When you have put yourself in the picture, study its general features and understand them.

Ask yourself about the causes and consequences, and about how that part relating to the future might change.

An academic insisted on having a ruler. Some people choose to draw a picture of a landscape, a city, a railway track, or other scene, and trace the progress of their life through what they have drawn. Others do strip cartoons. Some use a lot of thought bubbles or captions. Some do a series of pictures across several sheets of paper.

If you have never done this kind of exercise you may feel self-conscious. Remember this need not be a work of art – as a start, a sketch on the back of an envelope might be all you would wish to produce.

Jeff: *We were tempted to illustrate here with our own lifelines. But when doing this exercise independently – not for the first time, but each time it's done something fresh comes up – I found that I produced sets of pictures, links, and labels that were a lot of fun for me, and enlightening too, but they were not possible to condense within the format of this book.*

Christina: *I found that, too. Although I'm sorry to have my 'Game of Life' (Snakes and Ladders) collage left out! For me, the important thing when doing this is to give yourself lots of space, big sheets of paper, and plenty of colours to work with. But perhaps if you're doing this for the first time you might prefer to start with the back of an envelope and begin with a sketch in black and white.*

- **Exercise 3**

  Describe two events or episodes in your life that you now recognise as having been a turning point, when you made a decision that took you in a new direction. Select one that you feel turned out well, and one that did not turn out so well. How did this come about? What did you do? What are your thoughts now?

Christina: *The best decision I ever made? This has to be staying in London for Christmas in 1997. I stayed with my brother and went to have lunch with friends of his. I met a wonderful man who is now my partner. It took me in a totally new direction – Sydney, Australia. That was really because I wanted to do something different that year. I didn't have any expectations, yet that one meeting changed so many things for me.*

Not exactly a good idea: putting my money belt inside a handbag on holiday. Getting everything stolen (plane ticket, money, passport), and spending the rest of the holiday with the tourist police. I can't go back and change my actions, but it's taught me a lesson. We stayed in the cheapest hotel we could find. It was a real dive. It made me appreciate what I have got so much more, as well as developing the ability to transcend the physical environment at times (useful at the dentist's). It took a while to outgrow the 'irresponsible' label.

Jeff: *Going to university – rather late in the day at 24 – was a good move. I'd seen school friends come back as more interesting people with ideas that were new to me, and they were full of stories about university life. I thought: 'I want some of that.' Because I'd been supporting myself for more than three years since school I got what was called 'a major county award' for £360 a year that was real money in those days. I was most impressed – a life of sheer pleasure and they pay you, too!*

A few years after that I was offered a job in Nottingham working with David Smail, who would have been a fine mentor. But I turned it down because on a technicality the health authority wouldn't agree to upgrading me (that would not only have given me a pay rise but also have entitled my family to have our removal expenses refunded). I got myself in a huff, and went off to Oxford where they gave me what I had wanted (but maybe not what I needed).

- **Thinking point**
  In doing these exercises it is usually the case that each person gets some food for thought in making at least one discovery about self in relation to others. It may be a particular memory that has come to light, an emotional reaction that you had discounted, a different viewpoint, or a fresh insight. Allow yourself to chew over what you have found, and ask yourself what it tastes like.

Chapter 7, 'Developing skills', will describe Mode 3 functions and aspects of review in counselling and psychotherapy.

Chapter 7

Developing skills

SUMMARY Mode 3 skills build on those identified in the previous chapter. They include: self-preparation; choosing and framing questions; bringing the narration back to the present; involving friends and family; group work; pinpointing critical incidents; understanding the storyteller's stance; extending the range of media to be used; identifying and feeding back characteristic words, metaphors, and actions; working with dreams; analysing life scripts; enhancing commitment to progress; concluding review; and follow-up.

Narratives that are highly personal and often painful are the subject of this chapter, which presents ways of building on the preceding chapter to become more resourceful in review in general, and particularly in Mode 3. Concepts and methods from selected assessments and therapies will be introduced. These are not called life review but have a clear family likeness.

First a challenge, then a caution. The challenge is from Guggenbuehl-Craig (1991), who asks why narrators should expect compassionate understanding to help them towards serenity. If we find existence painful, that's just the way we happen to be, he suggests. This is it and that is that. On review for older adults he suggests that the best that can be expected is healthy debunking and developing a sense of humour to cut through myths that make existence seem more important than it is.

The caution is that, while the listener needs to be aware that to reduce a narrator's self-blame is one of the most important targets of review, the retrospective self-blame and guilt may be well founded. Sherman (1991) points out that feelings of guilt and remorse may be reactivated in review when a person has done wrong in the past to a loved one. If the loved one is dead, it is not surprising that the narrator feels it is impossible to make amends or be forgiven.

The storyteller is not mistakenly attributing guilt with distorted over-generalised recall, so a counsellor cannot appropriately confront and challenge the attribution that has been made. To do this, Sherman considers, would tend to make matters worse by making the client cling to guilt all the more firmly, and lose confidence in the counsellor. In such cases it is necessary to hear the client fully and completely, before exploring the probability that what was done was not unforgivable and inhuman, but unfortunate and all too human. Realism and compassion are called for.

Describing the position of specialists in developing the therapeutic use of reminiscence, Webster and Haight (1995) note that these are likely to become increasingly absorbed in specific ways of thinking and working. They tend to lose sight of other angles of approach, and profess that they do not have time to scan literature that does relate directly to their own current research interests.

Preparing yourself

Therapists understand the need for the listener to be aware of their personal story's influence and how this can affect listening and responding to narrative. Traps for the would-be therapist include: being prejudiced either for or against the narrator; encouraging dependency by prolonging contact unnecessarily; playing guru; and vicarious risk-taking through the narrator. A professional story about counsellors, therapists, and their clients is unwinding in the background to therapeutic listening – problems and their solutions are being considered by the practised listener at the same time as the story is being heard. The skilled listener is dealing with two stories in parallel, keeping the client in the foreground, while avoiding prematurely imposing definitive readings or meanings.

An important element in preparation is determination to say relatively little and to phrase what you do say clearly without psychobabble. Self-disclosure needs to be highly selective and always for a purpose, unless the listener is working as a partner in a co-counselling framework. Knowing when not to speak can be crucial when loaded memories emerge and the narrator needs space to decide whether to go on.

Framing questions

McAdams (1997) offers a semi-structured format, which we find useful and recommend as a basis for Mode 3 review.

Create a life book and its chapters. Think of your life as an unfinished book to be divided into chapters (at least two or three, and not more than seven or eight). Give each chapter a title and describe its contents and the transition between one chapter and the next. Present an outline rather than the whole story.

Pinpoint eight key events, providing as much detail as you can on: setting, those involved, what they did, and appeared to think and feel. The events: a peak experience; a nadir experience; a turning point; earliest memory; an important childhood memory; an important adolescent memory; an important adult memory; other important memory.

Select four significant people. Give details of your relationship with each and the role of each in your life story. Also describe any heroes or heroines you have.

Plans and dreams for the future. How will these affect: your creativity as an individual; and your ability to contribute to others' welfare?

Conflicts, challenges, stresses, and problems. Describe two current examples from this general category that are affecting you. How are you dealing with each, and what plans do you have for tackling them in future?

Personal ideology. Beliefs about: god or a guiding principle and religion. Do you have any special beliefs, and how have your beliefs changed over time? What about your political orientation? Your most important personal values?

Looking back at the book of your life, what is its central theme?

Questions, questions

In Mode 3 we recommend a 'rewind' approach starting with the present, rather than the chronological working-through favoured by Kimmel (1990) or Haight and Webster (1995). When the narrator keeps returning to material from the past and dwells on it, the listener in Mode 3 is well-advised to use prompts, repeatedly if need be, to bring the story back to the present.

'And how is this affecting you now?' 'What would have to happen for you to see this differently?' 'Truth can change over the years – what is your truth about this now?' 'How might you become able to change your mind about what seemed to be going on then?' These are phrases the Mode 3 listener can use in such situations.

The narrator asks questions as well as answering them. Characteristic pressing questions come up repeatedly in the course of some narratives. The listener is likely to be pressured into providing answers to these, but this should be resisted. A classic example is the question 'why me?' briefly referred to in the previous chapter. Some narrators ask this repeatedly, and it can become most tempting to respond 'why not you?' This would be unwise; it sounds like emotional rejection rather than enquiry, and more importantly it misses the point.

June, 52, went on a weekend visit to friends far from her home. Her husband, an invalid, 'begged' her not to go, his usual reaction. She went anyway and within a few hours of her arrival a message came that her husband had collapsed. He had tried to summon help but neighbours reacted slowly, and by the time help arrived he had died alone. For the two years that have elapsed since his death June has 'seen' her late husband several times. She continues to ask herself and others 'why?' questions. 'Why didn't I listen?' 'Why did he die?' 'Why did this have to happen to us?'

In her mind the questions have already been answered many times over. 'I was thinking of myself'; 'I wasn't there to save him'; 'it happened to punish me for being bad'. Instead of continuing to ask 'why me?' the narrator might be asked to think of her favourite question as the suitcase she took with her on the fateful visit. Now it is getting too heavy to bear because a lot of dirty washing has been stuffed into it over the years. She can then be encouraged to unpack the questions as she would a suitcase, to see what it contains that can be disentangled and sorted out.

Review can proceed to examine the evidence for and against each of the charges June has made against herself, and understand how it is that she has chosen to blame herself for that weekend's events and so many happenings in the course of her life. Joining her in a search for release, the listener will look with June for other statements that could work better for her.

Avoiding labelling

Showing negative bias in memory, a depressed individual is likely to focus on unhappy memories. The listener has to learn to become comfortable with interrupting and restructuring global negative evaluations ('nothing works', 'I'm a failure', and so on), while remaining sensitive to the narrator's independence. Not only is a sense of shared commitment needed, but also a steady refusal to get pulled into categorisation or labelling of any kind.

Family stories

Greene (1982) shows that a family dimension may be built in, reporting a case study of a daughter encouraged to be present at her father's life review and to respond to content bearing on their relationship.

Mouratoglou (1991) advises that listeners to older couples can feed back to each partner the story of their lives since childhood. Agreements and interpretations between individuals and their current families as well as their families of origin are important features of such stories.

Therapists can then proceed to elicit the couple's current dilemmas regarding changes in their contracts with each other. Tasks for them to experience the impact of new rules or agreements can then be set by agreement. In the course of therapy, family stories emerge, going back several generations, about conflicting stories that appear to have 'lost the plot'.

Group work

Therapeutic groups enable older adults to transcend preoccupation with self and see a wider meaning in life (Young and Reed, 1995). Intense personal reminiscence shading into life review is an important strand in the process of group therapy, and such groups can offer a more accessible way of developing insight into self in relation to others. Lesser *et al.* (1981) note that when a member begins individual life review the group's reaction is to put together a synthesis of legend around such themes as first memory, first day at school, or first dating experience. The value of peer support is urged by Brink (1979), who recommends that the group should be structured so that the narrator will receive positive reinforcement for recounting instances of effective coping, and non-reinforcement (but supportive encouragement) when describing ineffective coping.

Critical incidents

The narrator can often be assisted to track back to discover an early experience deemed to have been critical in causing a current problem. It is sometimes very slow work but they are usually sustained by the need to make sense of experience.

Feeling 'different' from other people preoccupies Emily at 79. She gives an example. One of a family of thirteen, she had always felt different, and almost invariably managed to keep out of family photographs even as a child, because she 'didn't want to be associated with them – it sounds awful, but that's the way it was'.

Emily can remember very little of her childhood, and she has 'no time for analysis and all that stuff'. Angrily, she changes the subject. But Emily perseveres to bridge the sessions, and at the penultimate session her first words are: 'I remember . . . I remember being out with my mother one day just before starting school. It was so rare to get her to myself. She met this woman, and them talking. Looking at me. And I remember Mother saying: "This one? I borned her myself. No one by."'

'I asked what "borned" meant and she said I shouldn't have had my ears flapping and listeners never hear good of themselves. The other woman looked down at me and said she was right. I felt ashamed and it just seemed to grow and grow. I was reading fairy stories at the time and thought I was a kind of changeling or something like that. It's always been with me – at the back of my mind. Something rotten in me.'

It is by no means guarantee of progress if the narrator is able to make such a discovery, but it can open up lines of enquiry that at the very least give room for hope. Emily was able to become more confident and active in meeting other people, having recalled her fear and having set it aside as no longer relevant. Historical objectivity is not paramount in such cases. A listener should appreciate that the content of such 'retrieval' may not be accurately recalled, and may be imagination, but if it works and the storyteller finds relief, that is what counts.

Scenario 17

Joe, who had taken early retirement in his fifties to devote himself to gardening after depression had led to a suicide attempt, is sensitive to any possibility of rejection. If his ideas are not well received at a parish meeting, if his partner contradicts him, if a shop assistant does not respond to him promptly – on such occasions he responds with extreme hurt and rage which he struggles to defend but eventually acknowledges to be disproportionate. Where does this anticipation of rejection come from, community nurse Zoe asks. Joe says he does not know. He thinks 'people like you' should be able to find out.

- **As Zoe, what would you do in this situation to continue to assist Joe to answer your question himself?**

(See Chapter 9, p. 157.)

Taking a stance

Review may usefully selectively amplify early memories that a narrator recalls as being special, to understand how a characteristic stance came to be adopted, which is being maintained in the present, but may no longer be appropriate.

Dolly, aged 69, has suffered a series of severe strokes and is 'marooned' in residential care where she is twenty years younger than the average resident. She is singled out by carers as the most 'difficult' resident because of her frequent complaints about the quality of their attention. Some of them strain to give her exceptional care and at the end of the shift ask her, 'How was that, then?' Dolly's invariable reply is: 'Rubbish!'

Describing how she is 'the baby of this establishment', she recognises that it calls to mind her life as a toddler. When she had finished a drink she usually threw the glass to the floor. 'I thought if I had finished drinking from it, it was no good to me any more. My mother used to say I cost her a fortune in glasses!'

Dolly is encouraged by her listener to relate the position she took up as a child in her relation to her mother, and her current stance as a 'me against them, most difficult resident', confronting her carers. The carers are also involved in understanding this story, and this becomes a way to work with Dolly and her carers to resolve the conflict between them. They are also assisted to stop competing against each other to look after her in an exceptional way, and to aim for care that is 'good enough'.

Varying the media

Sometimes words get in the way of feelings, and if you suspect this is happening the media used in review can be varied. Some people more readily relate through music, and a Desert Island Discs session or an impromptu recital with narrative interludes – a kind of karaoke – may result. For those who prefer visual communication, a picture or a series of pictures can be 'commissioned'. Lewis and Butler (1974) propose a wide-ranging choice. They list: written or taped autobiographies, with feedback that may include self-confrontation in a mirror, listening to tapes and picking up areas of conflict, boring and repetitive elements; pilgrimages; reunions; genealogy; scrapbooks; photo albums, old letters, and memorabilia; summation of life work; and exercises in preserving ethnic identity.

Chubon (1980) introduces the theme of relating to a novel – reporting a case history in which a client was prescribed the reading of a novel with several similarities to her own life, reviewing the book in relation to her life in subsequent counselling. Listeners are also viewers, able to add video, and computer-aided presentations with digital imagery. Idea processors, combined with word processors and graphics programmes, facilitate therapeutic life review (Reinoehl *et al.*, 1990). Software programs for qualitative analysis of transcribed interviews enable detailed study of emerging themes and interrelationships between ideas.

Hargrave (1994) uses video reviews with older adults. These are edited into vignettes of between five and twenty minutes, selecting a particular life stage or episode, and combined with family pictures and music. He describes the goals of this approach as being: to enable the family to confront with the past in an organised and constructive way; to help the family attach specific meanings to past events, clarifying long periods of family history and interaction; and providing a record. He reports that this multi-media approach triggered positive emotional responses in family members who had become accustomed to hearing stories, and viewing displays of family photos, over the years, but who found that this format made these things 'come alive'.

Bazant (1992) reviews uses of music in reminiscence for a number of purposes: to set a mood as a group gathers; to be used as a session topic; and to focus on the existential message in song lyrics. She notes that it is common for individuals to have a tune of special significance, with an emotional response having been learned by association during a meaningful episode. Davies (1978) describes an example of such learning as the 'Darling, they're playing our tune' phenomenon (DTPOT).

From time to time it can be constructive to prompt a narrator to describe their story with one or more self-selected analogies relevant to the individual or group. A life may be viewed as a house or a garden, a knitting pattern or a pools coupon . . . a wardrobe or a game of football. A reader might choose, 'if my life story were a book, what kind of a book would it be?' Or an enthusiastic cook might select: 'What kind of a meal . . . ?' There are many ways for a narrator to make concrete a picture of a life by opening up a fresh perspective. Films are a popular choice. Murphy (1996) has analysed *The Wizard of Oz* to point out how it elucidates difficulties met in our society and how they are tackled in course of development and change.

Scenario 18
Tom, a 24-year-old in a media studies department, who is in difficulties at college because he is frantically juggling too many commitments, chose a film immediately, picking Loony Toons. *He explains to his counsellor, Lisa: 'Everything moves very quickly, it's all very colourful, there's a cat or a dog or something that keeps getting chewed up or splattered and the next moment it's running round again alive by some kind of miracle. That's me. One day, I'm going to run out of lives. What do I do then?'*

- **In Lisa's place, how would you help Tom to develop what he is saying and examine its implications for his life as a student?**

(See Chapter 9, p. 158.)

For narrators who are ill at ease with words, features of their environment can be used to cue review. It is not uncommon in the process for the person spontaneously to turn out pockets, delve into wallets or handbags, or conduct tours of their home and neighbourhood, as part of demonstrating 'this is who I am'. Sometimes a story can only be grasped within the narrator's own surroundings.

Fifteen-year-old Stan is 'going nowhere' in his studies at a comprehensive school. His teachers get nowhere either in their attempts to counsel him. His parents blame the school for failing to do its job, and criticise their son for letting them down. Discussions at school end in recriminations and in sullen silence from Stan, who at the best of times is laconic and when pressed to speak expresses ideas hesitantly. Early one evening, the year-tutor visits Stan's home, by appointment, to find that the parents are not in. With a hint of a grin, which draws attention to a smudge of paint on his face, Stan reports that they have 'given me up as a bad job'.

The teacher comments on the paint, and eventually Stan agrees to show him 'my studio', a ramshackle shed at the bottom of the garden. For the first time, the teacher sees the abstract paintings Stan has been doing for the last four years – 'when I'm doing these, I'm happy – the only time really – they think I'm a nut case. When I get out of your place I'm going to art school – you can't stop me.'

Words and actions

A narrator's language gains from interpretation. For example, a man in his eighties responds to a greeting from his young listener by sighing: 'I'm panned out.' Neither of them knows the roots of this metaphor, but together they allow curiosity to overcome ignorance. They discover the rich meaning of looking over the narrative as the flow of a stream where there could still be some gold dust to discover. The active listener needs to be aware of characteristic words or phrases used by a narrator which require picking up and inspection in order for the story to move on. They function as passports. Repeated use of 'in only' is a case in point.

Leah, a 74-year-old widow, is emerging from the shadows of a fifty-two-year marriage to a self-styled 'long-standing anxiety neurotic'. In the early stages of bereavement she becomes preoccupied with self-blame: if only she had picked up the warning signs during their engagement; if only she had been stronger perhaps he would have become strong; if only she didn't feel so helpless now, when she was free at last. Her listener allows Leah to tell her story, then finds himself beginning to listen a second time around.

The listener intervenes and seeks Leah's view of the usefulness of 'if only' for her. Leah says that she has noticed her habit and it irritates her too, but 'it just slipped out'. The listener says they need not 'irritate' themselves any longer. She asks Leah to construct with her a conversation avoiding 'if only' and similar expressions, and relying solely on present and future tenses. Every time Leah uses 'if only', the listener will highlight it, repeat the phrase with emphasis, and request re-phrasing. Leah struggles to master the new way of speaking, eventually succeeds, and later is to identify this exchange as a turning point in her review.

Scenario 19

Mel, 37, who is a car worker, is due to lose his job with closure of his factory. He will not face the steps necessary to arrange retraining for other work. When the topic comes up with Trev from Personnel, Mel looks uncomfortable and keeps coming back to the same conclusion: 'We'll cross that bridge when we come to it.'

Bells ring for Trev, who knows Mel's father, who works at the same factory and will be retiring with the closure. He recalls that this phrase is often used by the deliberate and cautious older man. It sounds archaic coming from Mel, coming down with a clang every time to cut off discussion. 'More like a drawbridge', thinks Trev.

- **How might Trev and Mel work on how to 'cross that bridge'?**

(See Chapter 9, p. 159.)

Another way of becoming stuck in a story is when the narrator adopts a stance of confrontation in relation to others, and becomes so involved in what is going on that it becomes impossible, without intervention, to stand back and see what is going on.

Mo, a new charge nurse, was reflecting with her mentor on her frustration in failing to get the respect of her junior colleagues since she had been promoted. She did not know why they saw her as a joke. Why couldn't they understand her position? It was not fair. She was always bending over backwards to see their point of view.

Is Mo really interested in answering her own question? The mentor, like all good mentors, knows that questions are often rhetorical, with the questioner usually 'knowing' the answer. She invites Mo to turn her question into a statement: 'They do not understand me because . . .' Mo is unable to do this. She does not know how others see her. She wants to know. 'It might not be comfortable', the mentor cautions. Mo insists, so the mentor takes her to a room with a full-length mirror and asks her to assume her 'bending over backwards' position, hold it as long as she can, and describe what she can see from it. 'Only the ceiling', she puffs.

And how does she feel? 'Desperate – I'm going to collapse!'

The mentor invites Mo to sit down and asks gently: 'Mo, how did it come about that you think this is what being in charge should look like? Let's see if we can find a more comfortable way for you . . .'

This kind of approach can also be applied in structural family therapy. In family sculpting, members are encouraged to stage a tableau vivant, to present different coexisting perspectives of what is happening. For example, a narrator in the middle of family conflict, who tells her kin 'I seem to be pulled both ways at once', should be encouraged to act out what is going on and find out how this feels for the family. Use of metaphor is also important under this heading. Metaphors need to be reviewed as a story is re-told (Magee, 1991b). Trade in and trade up your old metaphors is a message to give narrators – with, for example, a woman choosing to graduate from pussycat to tigress.

Birren (1987) describes an insight, while teaching a university class in adult development and ageing in 1976, which led him to formulate guided autobiography. One day, as a change of pace, he gave students of life span development an unusual assignment. Each was required to write two or three pages of autobiography as if it were a tree, describing its major branching points; or as a river, telling how it flowed, narrowing and widening with events. The originality of their responses and the unusual level of excitement and interest generated by this project propelled Birren into rethinking his ideas about using autobiography in adult education.

Exploring a chest-of-drawers metaphor to examine the organisation of social roles, Eulert (1998) draws on her background as a drama therapist. She sets out seventy-two exercises for clients to learn how the social roles they play, and the 'masks' they wear in everyday life, influence their present behaviour, and can be expected to shape future action.

Dreams

It is not uncommon (Magee, 1991a) for narrators in therapeutic review to report an upsurge of dreams characterised by searching and seeking directions, and encounters with past situations that in some cases had been forgotten for many years. Brink comments that review is facilitated by dreams affirming life's richness and links of past and future.

Scenario 20

Elaine, at 24, is something of a paradox. The late-born child of middle-aged parents in chronic conflict, she had kept a low profile as a child at home, absorbed in computer games. Her parents did not have much time for her. Her mother, who was going blind, was preoccupied with herself, and her father spent much of his time looking for work, but with little success.

Mild-mannered and living alone, Elaine has lurking ambition, brilliant ideas, and works hard. She has the opportunity to expand her business interest as a partner in an Internet cafe, and is facing a major life change requiring her to assert herself and her needs more strongly than she has done for a long time.

She recounts to Frank, a psychotherapist, the return of a nightmare from childhood. 'I am approaching a dark tunnel that has opened up in the garden of my old home. I just know that I have to go down this tunnel and I do. I move into the darkness, convinced that there is some savage beast like a lion or a tiger but far worse cooped up. Just as I am beginning to wonder whether I might be mistaken, there is an almighty roar just in front of me and I wake up. Terrified.'

- **In Frank's place, how might you assist Elaine to discover what the recurring dream has to say to her?**

(See Chapter 9, p. 160.)

Scripts

Transactional analysis (TA) has developed the concept of the 'life script' (Steiner, 1990). This is a sense of identity and a constant orientation to others and the social environment, adopted in the first six years of life and likely, without successful therapy, to be performed to the detriment of the actor throughout a whole lifetime. The script's content, it is suggested, is based on a series of decisions taken by a child who, with the information at his or her disposal at the time, decides that a certain life course would be the best solution to an existential predicament. Like a tragedy, the script has a prologue, a climax, and a catastrophe. Its form is influenced by: the vulnerability of its 'actor'; and permissions (sometimes conditional) from adults. Script diagnosis as used by TA therapists can include many questions, and some of the most frequently used are posed in the exercise below.

- **Exercise 4**
  Answer two of the following questions. Consider how your answers relate to your life story.
  What is the family story about your birth?
  How were you named?
  What was your nickname?

How old will you be when you die?
What will it say on your gravestone?
What was your mother's/father's main advice to you?
What did your mother/father want you to be?
What do you like most/least about yourself?
Did you ever feel that something might be wrong with you? If so, what?
Describe the bad feeling you have had most often in your life.
What was your favourite childhood story/fairy tale/book/hero/ TV programme?
What would 'heaven on earth' be for you?
What do you wish your mother/father had done differently?
If by magic you could change anything about yourself just by wishing, what would you wish for?

Christina: *I was named after the Greta Garbo film about Queen Christina of Sweden. I always liked that reference. Claire also, because it sounded good with Christina. I was almost going to be called Kirsty or Catherine, but I'm glad I'm not. There were both of those at school but I haven't met many Christinas. I feel special and I can't imagine having another name. My nicknames were 'small face', and Christina sometimes shifted to 'crispy noodle' because I liked them.*

Jeff: *The family story about my birth was that it was touch-and-go. It was in hospital to be on the safe side because my brother not long before had been stillborn. The consultant was summoned in a rush, grabbed an apron, and rolled up his sleeves. I got stuck with the cord around my neck and after a struggle was hauled out. The marks of the medic's hands were on my face for some time and when my father first saw me he thought I'd be marked for life. My mother didn't see me for some time as I was whipped off to intensive care for some days, and when she did the marks had faded. No more children was the order, and their marital relationship changed in ways that weren't talked about, so it's still a mystery to me. The story left me feeling special in an odd way, something of a freak, wondering what effect it had, feeling responsible for change between my parents I didn't want to know about.*

Christina: *My favourite was 'Alice' because you used to read it to me and do all the voices. I had particular favourites like the Cheshire Cat, the White Queen, and the White Rabbit, too. I remember looking in the mirror and thinking that there was another world there if only I could get to it. The illustrations were wonderful and we had an old book that smelt just right too. It smelt like the bookshops on Charing Cross Road. My favourite fairy tale was 'The Snow Queen'. I remember that book too with the original drawings. I think the children were called Kay and Gerda. I read so much as a child (and still do). I'm like you, Dad: reading from the cereal packet if nothing else is handy. I had a bookshelf in my room. My heroines were Laura from* Little House on the Prairie, *Jo from* Little Women, *Becky Sharp, Elizabeth Bennett, and Jane Eyre. I was a Seventies child, which was the best time for TV. Favourite programme?* Tiswas. *A Saturday morning custard pie fight mayhem.*

Jeff: *Bad feeling . . . I would say something that as a child I learned to call 'howling darkness': HD for short. Surroundings took on the colour of an overcast sky, nothing seemed to mean anything, people around – if there were any – just droning on and on, but I could connect with anything they said. Being totally 'off message' and going up the wall at the same time. Haven't had it for more than thirty years, touch wood!*

Schema-focused cognitive behavioural therapy (CBT) also tries to identify and work on fixed and unproductive sets of assumptions concerning identity and social functioning formulated in early life. Narrators trying to discover whether they can identify a schema or schemas running through their story can be helped in this with a variety of exercises, and the following is an example. It is most useful with the storyteller who has real difficulty in getting to the point and keeps tailing off.

- **Exercise 5**
  Message in a bottle
  Try this in your mind's eye. You're marooned on a desert island. One day you see a bottle bobbing through the surf and you wade out to retrieve it. You know that inside there is a message that you first got long ago from your early experience. It is a belief about yourself in relation to others that shaped your early life. You break the bottle and read what is written on the spill of paper inside. What is the message? Who was the messenger? Do you still believe it? If not, what happened to change your belief?

Christina: *It's my basic belief that I struggled with for years – 'you don't deserve . . .'. I can't visualise it written down because it's inside my head. I only questioned it a few years ago. Other people deserved but I didn't and it served me right. Maybe because I was teased a lot at school. For being overweight, for being different. What's that quote – the past is another country, they do things differently there? It is the past but it had a big influence. The message is delivered by a group of children in a circle. It doesn't pop up any more, but I still struggle with saying what I want.*

Jeff: *The message is in my father's writing – tiny and spiky, crammed on the page and with additions in the margins – with my mother's signature as well in her rounded writing. It says that I'm all right but just in case they'll stay around to make sure. I used to wonder why they were reassuring me. I believe I'm all right, much of the time, and squirm less than I used to. They are still around in spirit, I feel, though they've been dead for many years. Now I don't believe my being all right is contingent on them, but I'm not sure, as far as I remember, that I ever did.*

Concluding

Review goes on between sessions, and each of these may end with a summary, including agreed targets for focused reflection to be explored before the next meeting and to be taken up then. The penultimate session may include a 'This is Your Life' presentation by the listener to the narrator, summarising their narrative as you understand it, and their plans to apply what they have learned. A written or taped record can be left for them to mull over and amend if required. As far as possible the presentation should be formed according to the narrator's production – the listener is a production assistant.

The final session may focus on celebration of the end of this stage of the narrator's journey, two-way feedback on the usefulness of the work done, and on planning for how they will continue under their own direction. Follow-up by letter or phone within four weeks, and by direct interview within three months, is to be recommended, as narrators often miss the close relationship. A development that has had positive results in our experience is to bring together narrators who have been working separately at the end of their one-to-one work, so that they can link up for continuing peer support if they want to.

Chapter 8 deals with 'Evaluation'.

Chapter 8

Evaluation

SUMMARY Evaluation issues relating to review used as everyday review, 'therapeutic' and 'educational' review, and as a therapeutic component are examined. Effects on symptom reduction, quality of life, and psychological adjustment are described. The value attached to review by narrators and listeners is considered.

Review is most frequently an everyday process. This is generally self-initiated, random and spontaneous, and unstructured, occurring naturally in the process of social learning. Self-talk may predominate and, for social comparison, dialogue with others, usually non-professionals, will feature. Its effectiveness tends not to be evaluated, as it is by nature difficult to measure.

Some of those who engage in everyday review may also find themselves involved in 'therapeutic' or 'educational' review (guided autobiography or history). This is usually semi-structured with narrators responding to a schedule of questions. Others (researchers, activity co-ordinators, or educators) generally initiate it. These programmes can include older adults both in the community and in day or residential care settings, people with learning disabilities, and patients in terminal care. This type of review is sometimes evaluated, and there is modest evidence that some programmes can lift self-esteem or mood state for some narrators, at least in the short term.

A therapeutic component of formulation and treatment in most psychological approaches to counselling and psychotherapy is a third mode of use. This is usually driven by the professional, although many clients and patients subscribe to the professional's assumption that the past sheds light on the present, and will do their best to work in partnership with the professional. The process takes different forms according to the theory the professional subscribes to.

It may be relatively specific in use – for example, in schema-focused therapy, 'life review' refers to a cognitive exercise that examines evidence that supports or contradicts a schema (a complex of ideas and feelings from early life which has an undue influence on current adjustment). Or it may be general and pervasive – for example, in existential counselling, review has a core function in establishing whether the client is living an authentic life, being true to self. Review as a component in counselling or therapy is rarely evaluated as such, because it is often embedded in a way that makes it difficult to analyse separately.

In this chapter are views and evidence on the evaluation of review in these different contexts, and ideas on how clinicians, researchers, and narrators might work together with a clearer sense of purpose. This should enable them to frame more useful questions and make sustained progress in their attempts to understand what works and how. Evaluation will be taken to include effectiveness not only in symptom reduction (where appropriate), but also in impact on quality of life and psychological adjustment. Issues relating to the subjective value attached to review by both narrators and listeners, and their perception of its relevance, will be considered.

Everyday review

Agreement that reminiscence is a beneficial activity is expressed by Costa and Kastenbaum (1967), Havighurst and Glaser (1972), Lieberman and Falk (1971), and McMahon and Rhudick (1964), among others. Reminiscence can contain the element of evaluation, but evaluation is not an integral part of reminiscence. The evaluation can also be internal and not shared with others and can occur at any time either during or after the reminiscence. Because it can occur in isolation the outcome is not always positive and there is not a lot of working through. The presence or absence of subjective evaluation in reminiscence is more dependent on personality traits of the narrator than on anything intrinsic to the reminiscence (Webster and Haight, 1995).

While a spontaneous review takes the form of a journey of self-analysis, this does not necessarily mean that everyone setting out on a review will be willing or able to enter or complete review therapy. Out of choice or necessity the process may not involve a therapist, or may be aborted for a variety of reasons, as there are many threats and distractions in any pilgrim's progress. Review has its splendours but also its miseries for the alienated individual who finds the struggle to confront existential isolation painful and sometimes unendurable.

A resource for well-being

There is potential for confusion in 'evaluation' being used in two senses (one process, the other outcome) by Haight *et al.* (1995). In the first sense, evaluation is described as the key factor in therapeutic reminiscing. They maintain that the narrator and the therapeutic listener have distinct tasks. The listener must guide the narrator to consider feelings and meanings. Questions should be posed to guide the storyteller to examine and evaluate the life event in terms of its emotional significance and its more general importance in the life story. In the second sense, Haight *et al.* use evaluation in a more conventional sense of appraising outcome. They found that a review group of women with an average age of 77 showed a significant increase in self-esteem scores, compared to results from 'attention' and 'no-contact' control groups.

Changes in perspective

Birren (1987) comments that humour in an autobiography is an indication that the writer has mastered a problem. He finds that, as people become more experienced with the autobiographical process, humour becomes more frequent. Its use suggests that the person has moved from seeing life as a series of problems to greater insight and mastery. However, while we find this observation to be generally supported in practice, much depends on the nuances of humour being used. For the narrator, wry self-deprecation can slide into bitter self-criticism; just as for the therapeutic listener the line between laughing with another and seeming to laugh at them is not an easy one to tread.

Birren and Deutchman (1991) report that positive outcomes include: a sense of increased personal power and importance; recognition of past adaptive strategies and their application to current needs and problems; reconciliation with the past and resolution of past resentments and negative feelings; resurgence of interest in past activities or hobbies; development of friendships with other group members; greater sense of meaning in life; and ability to face nearing the end of life with a feeling that one has made a contribution to the world. In a comparison of pre- and post-training data from forty-five participants, those involved reported greater self-acceptance and personal integration (congruence of real, ideal, and social selves), decreased anxiety, increased energy, and perceived themselves as more open to others.

Review is characterised by effort to evaluate the recalled memories in order to derive a sense of meaning and purpose to one's life. This entails working through painful emotional episodes as well as positive, self-enhancing memories. Evaluation involves renegotiating the meaning of memories, which can be complex given their origins in psychological, social, and cultural experiences. Seen from a current vantagepoint – perhaps a new construct system – previous sources of shame, guilt, and other negative emotions can be reconstructed in more positive terms.

A comprehensive review entails the recall, evaluation, and synthesis of positive and negative memories (Webster and Haight, 1995). Autobiography includes but does not require evaluation. It is difficult, if not impossible, to write about choices made in the course of a life without evaluating them. By virtue of the topics covered, evaluation occurs. It can take place in isolation, or shared with a group, to help the narrator reintegrate questionable events.

Interest in studies of reminiscence was stimulated by Boylin *et al.*, 1976, Coleman, 1974, and Fallott, 1980, Reports on therapeutic applications by Perotta and Meacham (1981–2) failed to find therapeutic effect, as did Sandell (1978) and Zieger (1976). Thornton and Brotchie (1987) in general have questioned the effectiveness of therapeutic reminiscence activities. They found that numerous group comparisons showed virtually no significant or consistent changes in the most obvious dimensions of improved intellectual, emotional, or social functioning targeted by group practitioners for their clients.

Scogin and McElreath (1994), with a meta-analysis comparing reminiscence-based treatments with results for no-treatment control subjects, show that if a study is well-designed and comprehensive in tapping the range of possible advantages of reminiscence it can have a positive outcome. Fry (1983), working with older adults with professional or managerial backgrounds and living in the community, offers an outstanding example. The subjects, who were screened for high levels of depression, showed substantial improvement in mood state following a programme that, using a medium of reminiscence and dream analysis, dealt with coping with painful feelings and negative life events, intrusive imagery and thoughts, anxieties and negative beliefs.

Life satisfaction

Sustained and successful effort to demonstrate significant gains in life satisfaction following review has been reported by Haight (1992), summarising three studies carried out over six years. The process involved a series of six one-hour counselling sessions based on her own Life Review and Experiencing Form (LREF) and (before and after counselling) completion of the Life Satisfaction Index-A (LSI-A) of Neugarten *et al.* (1961). In all studies an experimental group received review, while a control group had friendly visits without life review. The third study also had a no-treatment group receiving pre- and post-tests only.

Each of the studies was of a different population: elderly people in good health in the community; veterans residing in a nursing home; and participants who were physically disabled and depended on delivery of home support to enable them to continue to live in the community. Average age was 74 in the first two studies, and 76 in the third. In each, significant gains in life satisfaction were found for life review. Controls showed (non-significant) negative changes.

As Kastenbaum (1987) explains, it is difficult to evaluate therapeutic review strategies, for many reasons, including the lack of clear distinction between review *per se* and the variety of ways of engaging in general reminiscence that are used throughout the adult life span. In his opinion, clinical gerontologists who become advocates of this approach have let themselves be carried away by the best of intentions. They have seized an idea that sounds positive, and have rushed it into practice without careful evaluation – without recognising the need for evaluation.

The studies in this section present a mixed picture. The selection of criteria for evaluation deserves more thought. It is rare for narrators to be asked to nominate the benefits that they would hope for, and for researchers then to try to assess changes in those parameters in the course of life review activity. Also it is unusual for narrators to be asked for their reactions to the experience of review, to see to what extent the process is valued on its own account irrespective of subsequent outcome. Finally, it is extremely rare for members of the narrator's social network to be asked for their observations regarding the narrator's reminiscence activity, since so much of the material reviewed has a direct bearing on experience with family and friends and the way this is interpreted by the narrator.

Counselling and therapy

A post-modernist view of counselling and therapy would see the professional as a co-worker with the client, in a joint search for the social meaning created by shifting stories, alternatives, and identities. Rather than taking the perspective that the professional evaluates to present to other professionals, evaluation is seen as a matter for professional, client, and those close to the client to settle together.

For example, Lang and Lang (1996) describe working with Jewish families in which all the older adults are concentration camp survivors. Many of them have a struggle between remaining silent and talking, and the authors note that this is often paralleled within their families, where children pressure parents to communicate and parents are reluctant to do so. When a survivor becomes able to share with his family memories of a concentration camp, symptoms of post-traumatic stress, such as nightmares, are found to decrease.

> Formulation of the patient's problems, which the clinician derives through the initial assessment and at subsequent points during the course of an intervention . . . is the process of constructing explanations of current and past behaviour in terms of mental attributes, beliefs, emotions, goals and intentions – arriving at a set of hypotheses that offer a psychologically coherent model for the patient's problems, and which suggest the most appropriate mode of intervention.
>
> (Roth *et al.*, 1996, p. 53)

In the course of this process it is impossible to omit review, and clinicians are not to be differentiated as those who are 'for' review and those who are 'against'. Differences are to be found rather in the importance attached to the process in the course of formulation, and the degree to which the hypotheses and intervention modes referred to draw on review concepts.

Review is a deep-rooted component of many schools of counselling and therapy, and as such appears to have been taken for granted and not seen as requiring separate evaluation, so that specific investigation of its effects has been relatively neglected. Reminiscence itself has been evaluated, but, as Santor and Zuroff (1994) have indicated, accepting the past (a core component of ego integrity) may be unrelated to reminiscing about the past.

Coping competence

Defining review, we have proposed that a positive outcome would be assessed in terms of resolution of conflicts and improved well-being based on a sense of self-acceptance and having come to terms with life. We find the main functions of successful review for the narrator to be enhancement of: a sense of being in control of one's own life; understanding self in relation to others; and enjoyment of life. Illustrative comments from post-review interviews include:

'I've come to appreciate that I'm a bit of a rebel and it can be quite fun. To realise I'm not in a strait-jacket although I have been at times. I've got a bit of spunk. Something gets me going and I want to sort it out. I was in a sausage machine but I'm bursting out of it. I'm getting more confident by the minute.'

'It's new for me to be deliberately distancing myself. Saying, "I could be over there, being involved, but I'm not because I need to be self-protective". And this is the first time in my life that I've taken that kind of step, you know, which is good. I'm glad. I am. I feel that's a positive thing that I've achieved.'

'I can just go upstairs and lie down on the bed for an hour. I don't go to sleep but I feel so relaxed and so glad to be lying down. One time I would have thought "this is really old – lying down in the afternoon". Now I don't care – if we lived in the Mediterranean countries we'd be doing that sort of thing all the time, wouldn't we?'

Typically narrative alters in the course of review. Vocabulary changes with reduced usage of killer phrases, such as 'if only', 'if it wasn't for . . .' and 'yes, but'. There is reduced reference to past, particularly its more remote sectors, and correspondingly increased reference to present and to future. Many of the narrators are viewed, by the family member or friend they nominate as their closest person, as having become a more rewarding relative or friend to spend time with. In relation to life skills used in leisure or at work, the majority report that they have taken up new projects or have re-started projects that had been neglected.

Positive results with single cases have been described. Wasylenki (1989) reports alleviation of sexual dysfunction in a businessman, following life review focused on the evolution of his sexual identity.

Negative outcomes do not appear to be recorded. While it is extremely unusual for negative results of any therapeutic intervention to be circulated, the screening procedures called for in the literature would be expected to reduce incidence of such outcomes.

Lewis and Butler (1974) describe as possible outcomes of life review therapy, regret, anxiety, guilt, despair, and depression, but it is not clear to what extent, if at all, they experienced their patients as responding in those ways. They caution that the individual may become terror-stricken and even suicidal, concluding prematurely and without reference to the therapist that life has been a total waste – but they do not indicate how frequent such termination was in their experience.

Similarly, Verwoerdt (1981) reports that the results of review may range from nostalgia to severe depression with suicidal tendencies, without indicating the proportion of cases he encountered at the negative end of this spectrum. Kastenbaum also talks in general terms about the risk of encouraging life review in an 'obsessive' older person given to undue self-reflection, but does not give evidence that his misgivings are grounded in fact.

Health and behaviour

Rybarczyk (1995) claims that patients awaiting stressful medical procedures benefit from a prior opportunity for review. Two types of reminiscence interview are tested: one general; and the other including general reminiscence but also with about 25 per cent of its content dealing with successfully-met life challenges. Both types reduce anticipatory anxiety, and the second significantly improves patients' self-rated ability to cope and their reports of positive thinking during the procedures.

Pennebaker (1997) reports that studies of students describing a traumatic event, and past and present feelings in relation to that event, find at six-month follow-up an average reduction of 50 per cent in attendance at a university health centre, compared with those describing: a trivial event; just feelings; or just the event.

Disclosing deepest secrets could make us well, Pennebaker suggests, and, to probe the mind–body connection, he reports experimental studies in which students are asked to write in journals for fifteen minutes per day over a four-day period. Four conditions are compared: writing about a trivial topic; venting feelings about a traumatic experience; writing about the experience without expressing feelings; and describing both the traumatic event and feelings.

In the last-named condition, the students are instructed to write continuously about 'the most traumatic event of your entire life – something that has affected you very deeply'. They are asked to note all that had happened, how they felt about it at the time, and how they feel about it at present. They are advised that ideally they should select something that they have not previously talked about to others in great detail.

Pennebaker claims that, although students in the fourth group are initially more troubled as a result of this exercise than members of the other groups, after four weeks they improve significantly, and at six-month follow-up they are substantially healthier than the others.

Summarising a range of investigations across various populations, Pennebaker notes clear-cut behavioural changes as apparent results of engaging in such review. Student grades improve. Unemployed people get new jobs more quickly. Employed subjects show reduced absence from work. Terminally ill patients appear more serene and accepting.

Conclusions

Review needs a more substantial background of evaluation. Molinari and Reichlin's questions from 1985 remain open. What is the optimal time, ideal frequency of sessions, type of content? What processes lead to what kind of positive (or negative) outcome? What older people can benefit? Does the nature of life review vary according to age? How is review experienced from the narrator's perspective? How does review affect reactions to ongoing problems?

Priority should be given to linking the last two questions, evaluating outcome with subjective and objective criteria. In view of the shortage of therapists, such a programme might include: comparison of outcome for group and individual life review; experienced therapists, trainees, and client's peers compared as facilitators; or a co-counselling approach in which pairs of older people exchange roles of narrator and listener, contrasted with client–therapist format. As Kastenbaum recommends, professionals working with life review are giving more critical attention to their basic assumptions, and to testing effectiveness of various applications. There are encouraging signs from contributors to Haight and Webster (1995) of a concerted response to his call for more careful evaluation.

Clinicians and researchers need to continue to work together to ensure that review's opportunities are extended more effectively to clients' advantage. Using qualitative analysis and working more closely with clients themselves (whose contribution to planning evaluation has been relatively neglected), we need to face three related challenges. These are: to refine review therapy so that its use becomes more focused; to investigate outcomes from the client's viewpoint; and to extend controlled studies of the effects of one-to-one in comparison with group therapy, peer counselling, and other cost-effective approaches.

- **Thinking point**
  From your point of view, how important is evaluation?
  What are your ideas on how it needs to be developed?

Chapter 9, 'Scenarios', describes options for prompts and questions in the twenty scenarios that have been presented.

Chapter 9

Scenarios

SUMMARY Ideas for responding to the twenty review decision points represented by the scenarios in Chapters 1–7 are presented. Themes include: handling choice; identifying unproductive patterns; reframing the past; healing old wounds; new identity; and motivation.

This objective of this chapter is to revisit the scenarios that have been used in Chapters 1–7 as illustrations and opportunities for learning, and to consider ideas on how the choice points they represent might be handled productively. For a variety of reasons, narrators sometimes do not proceed with review, and we have included a few examples to demonstrate this, as it is important for a narrator to judge when to refrain from review or to withdraw when the process has been started but comes to appear inappropriate. Nearly all the situations presented are drawn from our experience but we have made many changes to the context to preserve confidentiality.

We do not see the commentary on these scenarios as offering inexorable 'right answers', but rather as a means of sharing our experience of responses that could be useful in promoting progress at a particular point for narrator and listener. While each has its characteristic flavour, an overview of the content reveals characteristic themes.

Handling choice

Repeatedly, the listener and the narrator need to decide whether to follow up a clue that could yield a fresh perspective on a story. The option to play safe, settling for an established way of telling a story that is familiar and rolls off the tongue, is attractive on a number of counts. To think about changing even a small part of the narrative may seem equivalent to demolishing a house of cards – take one out and the whole structure falls. Perhaps this fear is one of the reasons why narrators sometimes appear to come to the brink (of looking at an inconsistency that calls for explanation, of adding to the agenda unfinished business that requires resolution), and then draw back.

Unproductive patterns

The narrator is encouraged to understand how being stuck in a rut or other kind of groove has come about, and to decide whether to become unstuck, and how this can be achieved. This should not be presented as pressure to change, but rather as an opportunity to draw on assets that have been there all the time but not used to best advantage. The narrator cannot expect to become a new person (unless they experience a spiritual revelation), but they may become able to reveal unique strengths or other resources that previously they had not used to good advantage.

Reframing the past

Life events at the time they occur are perceived, understood, and responded to in the light of the person's experience accumulated up to then. This frame within which the picture of an event is viewed usually changes over time, with the ongoing process of reflection and continuing narration. For example, as an adult, the storyteller looking back at himself or herself as a child may be enabled to reappraise the humiliations and injustices of that time from a mature perspective, in which they are reframed, viewed differently. Seen from above, a position of relative independence, past experience looks less oppressive than when seen from submerged dependence.

Healing old wounds

Some past experiences remain intensely painful, even from an adult perspective. Abuse and deprivation, whether in childhood or later, is all too frequent in the stories we have heard. Time sometimes heals, and many narrators have come to their own resolution by their own efforts and the support of others before they reach us, but it is not uncommon to find storytellers who blame themselves for what happened, continuing to rub salt in their old wounds.

New identity

A story is self-presentation, recounting 'that was where I've been, this is where I am, that's where I'm going to'. Narrators have difficulty from time to time in knowing who they are, owning up to responsibility for being the way they are. We often encounter storytellers playing 'if it weren't for you', blaming others for their identity problems (parents come under attack frequently). In order to develop a new identity, closer to presenting the teller as he or she really is, risks need to be taken by listener and teller, in abandoning 'let's pretend' and confronting 'this is it, and that is that'.

Motivation

Who is review for? For the serious listener, who is listening in the conversation with a purpose that is counselling or therapy, the task is riveting and is its own reward. For the narrator, motivation tends to be more fragile. Those who are entertainers will lay out a life with relish, enjoy admiration, and weave fantasy to keep the admiration coming. The perplexed, looking for something that seems to be missing, will find another search attractive, but may lose interest when this becomes uncomfortable. The chronically bewildered will have great difficulty in deciding whether review is necessary.

Scenario 1: Alice and Tilda (p. 6)

Alice: *My problem is I always end up going out with chaps who are less . . . mature than me. And I end up feeling bad.*

This statement may be self-defeating. It could simply draw Alice's attention to the 'problem', rubbing her nose in it and serving only to contribute to her feeling bad about feeling bad. To move beyond this and to know herself better, a narrator interested in change would be well-advised to unpack what she has said. She could ask herself: *What do I mean by 'problem', 'always', 'mature', 'feeling bad'? Let me understand what it is I'm saying about myself.*

In doing this, Alice might discover that she has an attachment to her 'problem'. In her view it could make her a more interesting person, as it is something to talk about with friends. Or she might find that the 'problem' has a positive side: she does not feel ready for a close relationship while she is still a student, and she selects 'chaps' who are not ready either. In trying to understand what she means by 'mature', she could come to see how as a mature person she could expect herself to solve the problem she feels stuck with. If a mature person can judge maturity in others, how is it that she fails to use her judgement until it is too late?

Looking at 'always', she might find that she is over-generalising, possibly through focusing on recent experience at university, which will not necessarily be a marker for the rest of her life. Terms such as 'every time' or 'always' in narratives need to be questioned, as they can sustain feelings of sameness and inevitability that confine the narrator to repeating the same story again and again.

Considering 'feeling bad', Alice could attempt to understand the nature of her hurt. It could be that she sees this as normal sadness, the price to be paid for having relationships that inevitably change over time, not always in a positive way. Or it could be that she feels herself to be 'bad' and in some way to blame for not having selected the 'chap' with more care, or for having failed to elevate him to her standard of maturity.

Once Alice has achieved a clearer understanding of what she has been expressing, she is in a position to ask critical questions. *This has been something I have done up to now. Who will decide whether I choose to go on doing this? I will, since it is my behaviour. What, if anything, do I want to change? If I opt for change, what am I going to do to achieve this; and how might others help me? Given that males may lag behind females in psychological maturity throughout life, I may always have to face this. So the issue may be how do I come to feel better about doing something that's going to be inevitable? What will the future look like?*

Such questions are constructive self-talk. A change of tense is a reminder that this is a review of past experience, not necessarily a predictor of future behaviour. The questions deal with self-efficacy, choice, identifying options, and accepting that life does not stop being problematic, no matter how 'mature' one is or may become.

Tilda, Alice's listener, also faces choices. Most immediately, she needs to clarify what Alice is asking for, and to ask herself whether she is willing or able to supply what Alice wants either now or later. If the answer to the second query is 'yes', Tilda needs to negotiate how further conversation might be set up.

Scenario 2: Joan and Liz (p. 22)

Joan: *I wanted to be carried. My parents refused and went up the hill by themselves, telling me to wait for them. I was terrified but I did so. I have no memory of their coming back, although they must have done, mustn't they?*

For the narrator to report finding herself exposed to feeling alone in the world, as others who had been trusted suddenly show that they won't always be around, is not uncommon in review. In Joan's case the separation was particularly painful. She had been the only one of ten children to survive infancy and she and her parents were unusually close and protective of each other.

At the same time, as a child, she felt responsible for her mother's suffering in the series of difficult pregnancies and still births in the years that followed her own birth. Her mother, she recounted, used to tell her after she came home from hospital: 'I couldn't have borne it if it wasn't for you.' Joan reports that, while at the time she responded to the hugs that accompanied this message, part of her picked up on the 'if it wasn't for you' and felt somehow that she was being blamed.

Thinking it through with the listener she feels that being left at the bottom of the hill was for her like being an unwanted baby exposed on a mountainside to die. 'A bit of me did die then, in a way.' From this point Joan is able to be more open about her fear of approaching death, and to make connections between this, her reactivated memory, and her clinging to the carers who she saw as being able by their presence to screen her from death.

A carer is co-opted in subsequent review sessions, which focus on how Joan and her carers could use this knowledge from the past to make adaptations to the care plan. A key feature is a move to a double room to share with another resident who had similar fears; and the reported 'demandingness' that characterised both of them is reduced.

Each is able to help the other in the tasks of everyday living to some extent, and to reassure the other about whether or not help from staff should be called for, and, if help is necessary, to engage the other in talk while waiting for assistance to arrive. Also, the staff's perception of Joan changed when they understood more clearly that she was not a unique 'problem', and how her background had shaped her 'difficult' behaviour.

Scenario 3: Ivor and Jim (p. 31)

Ivor: *My life? If you want to know about that, it's in my medical notes. Just look at those – that's all you have to do!*

Not all narrators welcome a listener with open arms. Individuals who are preoccupied with physical illness understandably see storytelling that does not focus on their favourite theme as a distraction. Ivor is hostile when approached to take part in review, because he feels this would be construed as a recognition that his illness was 'all in his mind'. He does not want to be 'psychologised': this would be a rejection and an insult. The GP explains that investigations into his physical state would continue, and that the review was a separate process that would not affect the investigations, and, reluctantly, Ivor agrees to talk further.

Reasoning that the whole of Ivor's life had not been encapsulated in medical notes, Jim finds that Ivor likes telling stories – up to a point. He relates tales of his skill as a footballer as a young man, and how in middle age he had won trophies with his pub team in bowling. A handyman and a caretaker, he has held a variety of ill-defined jobs for indeterminate spells, and is nostalgic about these and the respect and satisfaction he recalls from his employers. Ivor will not talk about life since his retirement other than to say that it isn't a life as such, without his health.

His illness has robbed him of his life, stolen it from him, shutting it away in the case-notes. If only he hadn't become ill, everything would be fine. A picture emerges of a man unprepared for retirement, with no appetite for life in his new setting, profoundly unhappy but unwilling to deal with his feelings because he is 'not a sissy'. He appears to have taken refuge in illness – although being ill was terrible, it was not blameworthy, and 'if only' those doctors knew their 'business' he could be cured . . .

Jim comes to recognise that review is not appropriate at this time for Ivor, who is using the sessions to reinforce his preoccupation with physical illness. He shares this conclusion with Ivor, who welcomes Jim's honesty, and yet, paradoxically, wants to continue their 'chats', because 'at least you're not a doctor and all those doctors they've never done me any good'. Slowly and painfully Jim negotiates a new format for their meetings in which they work out ways of 'self-doctoring' that Ivor can use to reduce some of his discomfort. Over time Jim is able to encourage Ivor to integrate with a small group of other residents who meet informally to discuss health issues, share ideas about folk remedies, and decry modern medicine.

Scenario 4: Margaret, Jane, and Judy (p. 41)

Margaret: *I've half finished my life story. It's in my box. When I've got it done it will explain everything. But I don't think I can finish it. My memory, you know . . .*

Margaret is 'fishing' here. It sounds as though she would like her daughter as amanuensis as well as 'remembrancer'. Unsurprisingly the daughter shows no inclination to do this. The listener also resists any temptation to step in to be a surrogate daughter. Instead, she asks them to work together with her on their joint family story, working back from the present, so that they can understand how the current situation has evolved, and decide whether they want to make it better, and how they would do this.

When they do, it soon emerges that, while the daughter admires Margaret's single-minded attempts to build her career in what was a man's world, she is consumed with regret that she was neglected in the process. She voices the suspicion that the manuscript has no mention of the family, and probably concentrates entirely on Margaret and her career. Margaret rises to this charge: the listener battles to help mother and daughter to communicate without coming to blows.

Judy is about to suggest that the session should be aborted, when Margaret does what Judy had been hoping for, but was reluctant to prompt. She reaches for the box and takes out the 'manuscript'. It is a folder containing a few hesitant notes of dates and places. On the first page is a dedication: 'To my daughter, who suffered with me in the struggle.'

Jane caustically adds: 'Still!' Margaret is silent.

Judy turns to her: 'Still', she repeats.

Wearily, Margaret nods: 'Still. Jane – I'm sorry.' Jane is open-mouthed at the unfamiliar word, and while she is silent Judy is able to express briefly that this is an important moment for them and to propose that they 'seize the day' to make more progress. Mother and daughter accept.

Scenario 5: Blodwen and Helen (p. 44)

Blodwen: *I called for my friend – she had a squint and she was smelly, but she was my friend. And we got the fish and chips and we shared it under a street light in the rain. And I was happy.*

A depressed person can, like Henry Ford in marketing the Model-T Ford, come across with the message: 'You can have any colour you like – so long as it's black.' In developing a dialogue, the listener will want to probe for Blodwen to recognise other moments of colour or light on the palette of her life.

Helen: 'That's good. And when was the next time that you were happy?'

Blodwen hesitates, but once she has made the first admission, another is easier. 'When I got married. It was at the Register Office and I'd made my costume – I was a dressmaker in those days. And one of the guests said I looked really nice. And I did.' The story develops from here and begins to take on a different balance, in which it appears that, apart from four episodes of depression lasting a total of three years, her life has been either 'all right' or actually 'good – nothing to complain about'.

In subsequent sessions it becomes clear for them both that the relevance of review for Blodwen's psychological treatment is that it yields material which can be used to challenge her depressive assumptions. It is also helpful in signposting treatment objectives, since she is able to recall how she behaved when life was 'good'. She recounts that Helen would know when treatment had worked because she would see Blodwen going out to the shops with her hair done, and she would be able to hear her whistling ('not with much tune, though'), because that was how she acted when life was good. These markers that the review has uncovered are included in the assessment of her psychological treatment programme.

Scenario 6: Morag and Bill (p. 49)

Morag: *You are too young to know what a sense of duty formed at that time really means to someone like me.*

This is a common reaction of narrators to a much younger listener. It is a realistic reflection of the difficulty that can arise when one generation tries to understand another: the past is indeed another country. However, such a response may have other functions: it tests how the listener reacts to an obstacle; it asserts control – 'this won't be as easy as you seem to think'; and it expresses misgivings about the usefulness of review, asserting anticipation of unbridgeable distance between narrator and listener. Also it is a piece of special pleading, saying in effect, 'I was shaped this way *then*, and it's too late to do anything about it *now*'; and it can be a smokescreen hiding secrets the narrator does not want to reveal.

A listener can reply by acknowledging possible difficulty and asking for the narrator's help: 'Yes, it won't be easy for me to understand. Could you help me? I'll do my best.' This type of reply is usually effective in getting the story going again. If the narrator's response is repeated, the listener would be well-advised to make a similar reply and be prepared to do so several times.

While, in the course of our experience, the majority of narrators who have raised the 'you are too young' argument can be persuaded that relative youth is not an insuperable barrier to being able to listen productively, a listener's openness and patience are not always rewarded. If the narrator persists in maintaining 'you won't be able to understand', the listener will have to raise the other reasons why the narrator is keeping up this stance. Success cannot be guaranteed.

In Morag's case, when she was persuaded to begin her narrative, her misgivings remained and continued to surface. It became apparent that her fears of the consequences of being understood were overpowering for her. She feared that she was going insane and that if she left her home she would be transferred to 'an asylum'. Only a fragmentary narrative emerged; and she withdrew from review.

Scenario 7: 'The Old Salt', Amanda, and Carol (p. 84)

Amanda: *He's never seen the sea. Not once in his life! Talked about going . . .*

Immediate reactions are likely to be mixed. They could include for Carol embarrassment at being caught out, and concern that colleagues who already may be sceptical about activity groups will have their doubts confirmed. She may also feel annoyance with herself for not having done a more thorough pre-group assessment, annoyance with the narrator for having 'made up' the stories, and doubt about the authenticity of other narratives.

Amanda could feel amusement at Carol's 'mistake', and relief that other people having heard her father's tall stories will realise what she has had to put up with. This could be mixed with sadness at recalling how her father was always wrapped up in his farming with little time to spare for her, and many other conflicting feelings.

For 'The Old Salt', if Carol were to see the group as requiring the truth, the whole truth, and nothing but the truth, his stories would not be called for, or curtailed if he attempted to join the discussion. On reflection, and subsequently in the group, it may come to be understood that most life stories are a mixture of fact and fantasy, and it might well be that this narrator has firmly persuaded himself that the events he is describing really happened. They could have become his reality and he has a right to this.

In any group those members who leave out fact could benefit from gentle but firm encouragement to include it, to know themselves more fully. Equally, those who omit fantasy can gain from listening to tall stories and being helped to bring imagination into play. The question is one of balance – what is told can have the quality of authenticity for the narrator, who is persuaded that this is what should have been and therefore this is what was, and in its own way such a story is worthy of respect. Gradually, Carol or other members might be able to ask 'The Old Salt' more about his life in farming and his family, finding out what the obstacles were to his having had a life at sea. They could explore what had shaped his attachment, and ask his opinion about the yarns and tall stories that sailors are particularly fond of telling.

Scenario 8: Harry and family (p. 86)

Harry: *It was unheard of for a Marine to do that sort of thing, unheard of.*

From further discussion with Harry it becomes clear that late in the day he is making restitution in saying 'sorry' to many people. These include his family mortified by his decision, and the officer who did what Harry and others might have wished to do. There were also those who died in front of his eyes and whom he was unable to protect, and his younger self who suffered in silence because Harry could not find the words and had himself been 'unheard'. This discussion over tea becomes an impromptu family review session.

Present is Harry's only sister, probably the closest to him of those who are left. When he finishes his account she responds instinctively by hugging him. Harry says little, but he exhales sharply and his eyes fill with tears. By the end of the session he has explained how he had felt to be 'a pretend soldier whose heart wasn't in it', and the listeners have shared the different ways in which they have felt the weight of their parents' expectations.

Harry reports that he feels a weight has lifted from him; but immediately begins to apologise for 'burdening' them in the process. His sister cuts him short: 'Don't be daft! What do you think a family's for?' Another listener notes sadly that in a lot of families – perhaps their own was one of these – each member bore his or her own burdens – especially if they were big ones.

Scenario 9: Louise and Heather (p. 88)

Louise: *I'm doing these things now because I know she would have hated it – we've lost touch now, but I know she would have.*

Louise is indeed concerned with relationship. She explains that her father lived a semi-detached life in the diplomatic service with frequent travel which took him away for long periods. Her mother was caught up in a social round of entertaining, and ever-changing brief affairs, while servants looked after Louise.

Her father was invoked by her mother (who saw her as out of control) to discipline her. He did so coldly without betraying any annoyance, which Louise always found frustrating. Her mother at least reacted so that Louise knew she had got through to her, but as time went by her mother became less and less responsive and eventually left home for another relationship.

Louise is left with a pattern of behaviour originally chosen on the grounds 'your mother wouldn't like it'. By now her prolonged adolescence of risk-taking of various kinds – sometimes enjoyable, sometimes shocking and painful for her – appears to have become functionally autonomous, detached from its original cause.

Any review stemming from this first memory could be expected to identify the setting out, understanding, and revision of this unproductive pattern as a priority. This should only be attempted if Louise wants that to happen, and if she can see Heather as not just another mother figure to scandalise and provoke to another rejecting walk-out, replaying history, so that Louise could say to herself: 'I told you so.'

This is the essence of Heather's response. Louise is furious and argues for most of the session that Heather has totally failed to understand her. Towards the end, she threatens to wreck the office. There are two empty coffee cups they have used on Heather's desk, and Louise picks up Heather's cup as if to dash it against the wall. Heather blinks (it is a cherished cup), but retains enough composure to comment: 'So now it's *my* cup's turn?'

Louise freezes as the realisation sinks in that they have circled back to the start of the story. She smiles playfully and shrugs: 'You win. When do I come back for more?'

Heather does not return her smile: 'You win – if you want to. And we've got another fifteen minutes to work with. We have to sum up and then decide what to work on next time. What's your hurry?'

Scenario 10: Gillian and Brian (p. 89)

Gillian: *He hasn't written for three months . . . How did I finish the last letter to him? I think I said 'don't come to my funeral' . . .*

Sometimes a story stops because people 'have words', thinks Brian, frowning unwittingly as he considers Gillian's answer. And sometimes a few words can stop a story in its tracks. Responding to his solemn expression, Gillian asks what is the matter.

'I wouldn't be seen dead with you', Brian says.

'Pardon?' asks Gillian, looking shocked.

'If I was your son and got that message from you . . . that's what it would sound like to me.'

Gillian shakes her head: 'No that's not what I meant. What I meant was that I'd love to see him again soon. I was saying please don't feel you have to wait until you have to come to my funeral.'

Brian nods: 'That was a lovely message. Especially the bits in brackets. You could have put them in, don't you think?' They discuss the theme of 'reading between the lines', and compare Gillian and her family and friends in terms of their propensity to be able to do this. In the course of this discussion Gillian acknowledges that there are many splits between members of her circle. One of these splits is between those who are refreshingly imaginative and able to take a flight of fancy, and others who are lovely people, of course, but infuriatingly literal, and who insist on 'having everything spelled out'. She acknowledges that she belongs to the former group, while her son is in the 'literal' faction.

However, she does not spontaneously make a connection between this information and her son's reaction to her message. Only when Brian has repeatedly urged her to look at her message through her son's eyes, does she begin to look thoughtful. At the next session a fortnight later Gillian mentions as an afterthought that she has sent another letter including 'the bits in brackets', and her son has already replied.

Of course, as a mother, she understands her son. You have to write to him in a special way. Brian congratulates her. Not every mother would be so considerate.

Scenario 11: Cecily, her mother, and Vicky (p. 90)

Mother: *Cecily! You'll never come to any good!*

Cecily reports that this message really 'sank in for me. She sounded so convinced and I thought it was self-evident. It stood out a mile.'

Vicky asks her to explain what she understood her mother to have been expressing. Momentary annoyance – or a life sentence? What would a suitable punishment be (if any) for being a girl, getting your dress dirty, and having a bruised knee? Was it possible that in the heat of the moment her mother had produced a verdict without considering the evidence?

Cecily is asked to play the role of prosecutor, while the listener takes on the conduct of her defence. They will exchange roles in due course, whenever Cecily feels like it. The review continues as a trial: at first solemn and voluble. Little by little the 'prosecutor' runs out of arguments and assurance, as the 'defence counsel' rebuts each point in turn.

After twenty minutes' debate, Cecily can't keep a straight face and has to ask for a recess. After the adjournment Cecily switches roles without notice and presents a fluent defence rejecting the charge. The new 'prosecutor' tries to interrupt, but fails to get a word in as her opponent is in full flow, speaking with growing confidence and excitement.

'What's happened?' Vicky asks when Cecily pauses for breath.

Cecily is exhilarated: 'I've just heard both sides of the case – for the first time in my life. I'm not waiting for the summing up. It's not guilty!'

Readers who are familiar with Gestalt therapy may recognise the flavour of this experiential approach. However, such techniques are widely used by life review practitioners who do not consider themselves to be Gestalt counsellors or therapists. None the less, they recognise that a story is not only to be told in 'I said, she said' form, but often needs to be acted out with involvement by the listener and narrator in order to have a more complete expression of important feelings.

Scenario 12: Jacintha, her husband, and Alan (p. 91)

Jacintha: *I blame the bus company. I blame the surgeons. I blame God. But angry with him? Me?*

Jacintha is going out of her way to deny an accusation that has not been made, in response to being asked how she now feels about the loss of her husband. This needs to be pointed out by Alan. Her residual anger could have a number of sources: her husband has had the last word; she feels she has been deserted; she feels responsible ('if only'); and because he looked after her with such devotion she sees him as having robbed her of independence. In producing a hit list of external agencies, she is signalling that, superficially at least, she is choosing to present their relationship in an idealised way, minimising the flaws that are inevitable in any relationship.

Alan tries to persuade her to challenge her own views in a number of ways. He proceeds to normalise her experience, making it clear that a bereaved person generally is left with mixed feelings. He encourages her to voice her emotions that she had been unable to express at the time because family and friends did not make themselves available in the months following her husband's death.

This is done in a series of meetings. These involve her only son Charles, other family members, and her friends, who are able to admit that they felt unable to respond to the mixed anguish and desolation she had presented since her bereavement, and unable to express how much they had been affected by the loss of her husband. Alan asks her to open up her agenda for life review.

Charles is encouraged to facilitate, not only because he was active in soliciting the session, but also because he offers another perspective on what happened between his parents, and will be involved with Jacintha in implementing any changes in her lifestyle.

Scenario 13: Michiko and the monk (p. 92)

Michiko: *Where was the mistake in my practice – where has it gone wrong that I should still feel this? If my practice had really borne fruit, surely now I should be able to face death with more equanimity and peace?*

The monk who listens recognises that the most useful response he can offer Michiko is to recommend a technique to practise that will help her to detach herself from anticipating death as a looming event. He tells her that our lives are truly sequences of discontinuity – repetitions of being born and dying in each moment, as we breathe in and breathe out.

Everything from the past that could be used for comparison has been swallowed up in a black hole. She should practise living and dying in each instant, without a future. He recognises that people who are healthy and getting on with their work might well laugh at this. But to an old woman suffering from cancer it is not a joke.

Michiko puts his advice into practice with great determination, living in each moment. Over some weeks of concentrated practice she gradually becomes released from her unremitting effort to try to do what was right. In the process, she relaxes into a younger and more open person. She had come to a level of playful understanding, not attaching value to what she did or being concerned with what others would think.

In hospital she astonishes staff by her interest in and concern for them. At first they are alarmed at the strange attitude of this dying woman. To her, they are all visitors whom she might never meet again, so she shows them tenderness. Her last words are: 'I have lived a very difficult life. I'm a little girl. Now I'm going into the forest to play with a ball.'

Scenario 14: Susan, Bob, and Terry (p. 92)

Bob: *I think perhaps, from what mum has said, the orphanage was quite strict and there was* (sic) *quite a few rules . . .*

Bob is encouraged to voice his theory that perhaps his mother, who is 'mixed up' in her thinking, has confused the nursing home with the orphanage of her childhood. She lived in the past, and in many respects, although he did not like to say this, was like a child. She had been 'put away' by her father, and now he, her son, had put her away too. So maybe she was going back to the past and feeling as though it was all happening again, because this was her yardstick.

Terry acknowledges that this is a reasonable hypothesis. Her night-time protests might indeed be understood in this way. For Susan it is possible that, particularly at nights when she was more tired and there was less to keep her attention occupied, she could react 'as if' she were still in the orphanage.

The hypothesis is explored when key workers from the care staff are involved in the review process. Previously hostile to Bob because they thought he was 'too involved' with his mother and unduly intrusive in helping her with toileting and bathing, they become able to plan with Bob and his mother. A focus of attention is how night staff may be prepared to react with more understanding, knowing 'where she is coming from' in making her night-time protests.

They note that if she is made comfortable at their observation station, with a pack of her favourite biscuits and a magazine that she is continually absorbed in skimming through, she is less restive, and gradually becomes able to appreciate where she is and who she is. When this fails they discover that if Susan accompanies one of them on an inspection round, and is given a commentary on what is being done and why, she usually responds at the end of the round by asking to return to bed, and settles.

Scenario 15: Len and Rose, Len's mother, and Sally (p. 94)

Len (echoing his mother's daily enquiry into his morning bowel movement): *Have you been?*

His wife had recognised immediately 'that's her!' He had captured (or been captured by) his mother's voice, and it was clear that the routine of interrogation was still alive. Len reported that he had been brought up in a time and place when it was considered essential for the well-brought-up child to have a bowel movement before breakfast.

If you didn't, the consequence was not only parental disapproval and cross-questioning, but also having to take what Len refers to as 'a dose of the jollop', a powerful laxative. Immediately Len touches on this topic, he is instinctively tightening his sphincter and re-experiencing the mixed anxiety and anger that had swept over him as a child when his mother's interrogation became insistent.

Recognising this, Len becomes able, slowly and with difficulty, to question his childhood conditioning and to understand that because of illness there had been a number of recent changes in his diet, in his pattern of physical activity, and in his mood state. To adapt to these he needed to rethink his mother's ideas about bowel regularity.

With wry humour Len recognised that he had 'swallowed' a good deal from his mother in terms of beliefs about what he should and shouldn't do, and Rose confirmed this. With Sally's help they were able to make a start on questioning the continued usefulness of some of these long-standing preoccupations.

Scenario 16: Dave, Glenys, Don, and Gloria (p. 95)

Dave (to Don, his father): *Stop winding me up. I'm not your dad – you're my dad! OK?*

Don: *OK, Dad.*

Informal carers of a dementia sufferer often report that they have no time to review the family's evolving story or to try to make sense of the changes that are taking place in relationships within the family with the passage of time. All too often, carers assume the worst, taking the reactions of the sufferer as expressions of an illness, or as wilful attempts to be difficult and cause them extra distress.

Gloria asks herself whether Don is responding in terms of a shift in his dependency, recognising that his child is now parenting him. Dave would be all too aware of his father's dependency, but has not yet achieved filial maturity (recognition and acceptance that he had become the parent figure for his father).

To test her idea, Gloria asks Dave to think of things he is now doing for his father that might give the old man the impression that he is being looked after like a son. Dave says he can think of nothing. Pushing for understanding, and looking for concrete examples that might be easier to process, Gloria asks Dave what had been the most recent thing he had done for Don.

Dave recalls that the previous night he had been at his father's house trying to settle the old man for the night. He and his wife usually felt more comfortable if Don was asleep when they left, but on this particular night 'he just wouldn't settle'. Finally, in desperation, Dave picked up the newspaper and read aloud to his father until the old man slept.

Gloria leans back: 'Well, then . . .' The penny still hasn't dropped for Dave, who leans forward angrily. His wife puts a restraining hand on his arm. 'I'll explain when we get home, dear.' Taking this cue, Gloria finishes the session.

At their subsequent meeting Dave is able to express his appreciation that his father has been expressing the reality of their relationship as he sees it, rather than 'winding him up'.

Scenario 17: Joe and Zoe (p. 120)

Joe: *I don't know where this feeling of rejection you're talking about is supposed to come from!*

'What ideas do you have?' Zoe asks.

Joe blames it in turn on the stress of modern life, on his early retirement, on anxiety about his failing health, and on his partner's lack of respect for him. Each of these supposed causes is examined in turn in the course of review, found wanting, and put on one side. Zoe wonders if his anticipation of rejection is like a weed with a very long root. Perhaps Joe could do what he did in his garden – put his back into it and dig a little deeper.

In the following session Joe begins by announcing that of course he knows what the cause is, and has known all along. He is not soft. The listener agrees that Joe is far from soft and asks to share the knowledge.

As a 4-year-old, Joe recounts, he had been walking to the village shop with his mother when she stopped to speak to 'a gypsyish-looking man'. She despatched Joe to play on a swing nearby. As he looked back and saw the two talking he 'knew' his mother was trying to sell him to the man, and wanted him out of earshot, so he did not interfere.

Joe explains that his mother was a single parent with two small children, and at the time the family were lodging in one room. Afraid that they might be evicted if the children played normally, the mother constantly hushed them into silence and threatened: 'I'll sell you to the gypsies if you won't be quiet.' Joe's sister 'just laughed' and was not cowed, but Joe took the opposite point of view.

'Me and my sister disagreed about everything anyway, so the more she said it wasn't so, the more I said it was. Also, Mum went to church with us three times each Sunday, so she couldn't have lied, could she?'

Zoe again asks Joe how he would answer his own question. Painfully, Joe manages to say that perhaps his mother had 'lied – to keep the peace', and as a child he had dimly recognised this but did not want to admit to himself that his mother was, as he saw it, unreliable. He visibly relaxes as he makes this statement, and the review is able to proceed to explore and test the other 'evidence' that Joe had gathered in the course of his life to develop the schema of rejection, and to balance this against evidence to the contrary.

Scenario 18: Tom and Lisa (p. 123)

Tom: *Everything moves very quickly, it's all very colourful, there's a cat or a dog or something that keeps getting chewed up or splattered and the next moment it's running round again alive by some kind of miracle. That's me. One day, I'm going to run out of lives. What do I do then?*

Exploring life in terms of a film (or any other form of metaphor) can sometimes enable the narrator to approach hidden concerns obliquely. Normally Tom is an entertaining storyteller who prefers not to touch on difficult issues. The first issue for Lisa is: does Tom want to answer his own question? After all, this is a question that never arises in the *Loony Toons* cartoons he is describing. The 'now' is insistent and strident: the future irrelevant.

When Lisa asks Tom why it has occurred to him to ask this question at this time, Tom looks thoughtful. The listener points out that is not a question that Tom (the cat) ever asked when he was being chewed up or splattered by the agency of Jerry. Has Tom had some chewing-up that has happened to him off screen, which has caused him to question his apparent invulnerability in on-screen antics?

Tom is hesitant for a long time, and then begins to describe a recent 'sticky situation' at the college of further education where he is a part-time mature student. Confident that he is 'fireproof' because he is more intelligent than his fellow-students, he has been falling behind with his work. His supervisor has told him he will be asked to leave, unless there is a dramatic and sustained improvement.

This isn't the first chewing-over Tom has been given in his life. Up to now he has been encouraged to think of himself as an under-achiever academically, and he has been almost proud of this aspect of his identity. However, the supervisor has challenged this view for the first time, suggesting that he does not anticipate that Tom has the intellectual capacity for the course, and is asking for improvement more in hope than in expectation.

Ruefully Tom admits that the supervisor's challenge to his assumed intellectual superiority has left him 'feeling flattened – like one of those cartoon creatures when it runs into a brick wall'. Lisa and Tom use this opportunity to begin to review Tom's experience of learning, and consider how he might adapt his study programme to (in his own words) 'escape from Disneyland – it's getting dangerous'.

Scenario 19: Mel and Trev (p. 124)

Mel: *Retraining? We'll cross that bridge when we come to it.*

Narrators uncomfortable about opening up their story signal their discomfort in various ways. Some become silent but engage in body language that can include characteristic displacement activities, gestures expressing their tension. The listener in these circumstances needs to be a careful *watcher* as well.

Others like Mel bring up a characteristic dismissive phrase. Often this is a worn cliché, but the narrator has chosen it. It has personal meaning and also perhaps meaning for the listener, who can use it to approach the narrator and conduct a dialogue in the narrator's terms.

For Trev, this phrase sounds strange coming from Mel: he associates it with older people. He knows Mel's father is retiring with the closure of the factory, to cross his 'bridge' into retirement at 59. Perhaps Mel is echoing his father, with whom he had a close and respectful relationship.

Trev begins to tell Mel a story about three people – Trev, Mel's father, and Mel – standing by their car on a road bridge that didn't immediately look like a bridge, while each argued about when they would come to 'the bridge'. There was such a road bridge close to the town, over the railway – it was possible to be immediately approaching it and even on it without knowing you had come to it. What would they do when they came to the bridge? Who would take the wheel and make the decisions?

Mel becomes drawn in to the story, and is able to take part in discussion, first as himself and then taking over his father's role and Trev's. For the first time he is able to voice his disappointment that his father, looking forward to his own retirement as a chance to spend more time on his hobbies, has been unable to take his son's perspective. He has only offered the phrase about crossing the bridge: Mel is repeating this because it has been the only expression of feeling sanctioned by his family. Trev is able to use this opportunity to indicate that Mel, perhaps for the first time in his life, has the chance to give himself permission to choose what he wants to do without waiting for his family to give him a lead.

Scenario 20: Elaine and Frank (p. 126)

Elaine: *I move into the darkness, convinced that there is some savage beast like a lion or a tiger but far worse cooped up. Just as I am beginning to wonder whether I might be mistaken, there is an almighty roar just in front of me . . .*

Frank suggests that the nightmare could be like a computer game, in that it has violent overtones but also offers an opportunity to learn how to come through violence and win. Each component of the dream may be understood as expressing a part of her and her experience. Bringing together each part and owning up to all her own feelings could be the way forward for her to continue exploring her world without undue fear.

Elaine is encouraged to recount the dream in first person and present tense. She is asked to enact in turn from different standpoints the explorer knowing that she just has to go on, the garden surrounding her, the dark tunnel, and the savage beast, and to reflect throughout on how each experience feels and what it communicates to her.

At first she has real trouble in identifying with the beast, producing a strangled sound like the yelp of a Pekinese. Frank needs to encourage her forcefully to become louder. She surprises herself and him by leaping to her feet, roaring, and launching herself across the room, stopping with her 'claws' just short of his face.

Both are shaken by this outburst. Trembling, Elaine explains how as a child she bottled up anger at her parents' lack of involvement, and chose to express it indirectly in fantasies and game playing. Frank acknowledges what she has to say and then returns to the present. He asks what the difference might be between the dream then and the dream now. Elaine reports: 'The only difference between then and now is that sometimes then I woke up and I'd wet myself. At least I don't do that any more . . .'

Frank looks with Elaine at other differences. She is 'not as terrified as I should be – startled but not scared stiff'. They consider that the re-emergence of the dream in a different guise is a reminder that she is actively planning to raise her profile, to wake herself up, and become a big noise. 'Was the world ready for this?' Frank asks.

Elaine laughs suddenly, in apprehension and excitement. 'It had better be!'

- **Thinking point**
  Compose scenario 21. Identify in your own life, or the life of someone you know well, a choice point that is waiting to be faced (a question to be asked, or a statement to be made, a decision to be taken, or an action to be carried out). Express it to yourself. Listen to how it sounds and take it in. Decide how to deal with the choice and move on.

The postscript introduces ideas for further learning.

Postscript

Resources for further learning to develop your appreciation of review are within you and all around you; and it would need another book to offer a comprehensive list. Here are a few sources that we have found particularly valuable as a guide and inspiration to us, and we hope that some of them will be of use to you. Many of them will be familiar to you already. Even with those you know, it might be worth taking a second look. Choose your own sources that have a particular meaning for your reminiscence and express important feelings in your own life regarding choices and transitions. Elicit narrators' choices if you are a listener and use them to enhance review. If you are teaching you will find that selective use of a few clips and quotations enhances presentations and engages learners to identify their own choices.

Further reading: Bornat (1994), Haight and Webster (1995), Sugarman (1986), Viney (1993).

Organisations: Age Exchange, The Reminiscence Centre, 11 Blackheath Village, London SE3 9LA; Oral History Society, Department of Sociology, University of Essex, Colchester CO4 3SQ.

Art: Tracey Emin, 'Everyone I've Ever Slept With 1963–1995'; the Picasso Museum; Rembrandt's self-portraits; Rodin's house; Stanley Spencer's Cookham paintings.

Autobiographies: Augustine, *Confessions*; J.-D. Bauby, *The Diving Bell and the Butterfly*; W.H. Davies, *Autobiography of a Supertramp*; C.G. Jung, *Memories, Dreams, Reflections*; Jack London, *John*

Barleycorn; Fritz Perls, *In and Out the Garbage Pail*; T. De Quincey, *Confessions of an English Opium Eater*; J.-J. Rousseau, *Confessions.*

Epiphanies (just one example out of many): Discovery of PCR (polymerase chain reaction) by Kary Mullis in May 1983. One second he was driving along Highway 128 in Northern California, watching buckeye blossoms illuminated on a warm spring night. The next he understood how to reproduce and distinguish DNA on a massive scale.

Fiction: Samuel Butler, *The Way of All Flesh*; George and Weedon Grossmith, *Diary of a Nobody*; David Lodge, *Therapy*; Tolstoy, *Ivan Illitch*; Kurt Vonnegut, *Slaughterhouse 5.*

Films: Bergman, *Wild Strawberries* and *The Seventh Seal*; *Groundhog Day*; Kurosawa, *Living* and *Rashomon*; Michael Powell, *A Matter of Life and Death*; *The Truman Show*; *The Wizard of Oz.*

Music: Judy Collins, 'The Circle Song'; Smetana, *Ma Vlast*; Kate and Anna McGarrigle, 'Talk to Me of Mendocino'; Edith Piaf, 'Non, Je Ne Regrette Rien'; Linda Ronstadt, 'Pancho and Lefty'; Carly Simon, 'Coming Around Again'; Frank Sinatra, 'My Way'; Lucinda Williams, 'I'm Going to Change'.

Appendix

Biographical interview (Kimmel)

How did your upbringing as a child prepare you for life?
What are some of the milestones that stand out in your memory as you look back over your life?
Have there been any other milestones that stand out for you?
What about crisis points? Have there been any crises?
If I were to ask you who you are, how would you answer?
Do you feel a firmer sense of identity now than you had before? (How has that changed? How has that come about?)
Would you say that you have changed very much over the last few years?
In what other ways have you changed?
Has your relationship with your partner changed in the last few years?
Has the way other people think of you changed over the years?
What have you learned from your life?
Do you sometimes look back over your life and review what's happened?
Do you have a sense of having achieved something with your life?
Do you sometimes think about death?
How do you feel about the future?
What kinds of things are important for you now?
Are you looking towards the future mostly, or thinking about the past, or just concerned with the present?

Life review and experiencing form (Haight)

Childhood

What is the very first thing you can remember in your life? Go back as far as you can.

What other things can you remember about when you were very young?
What was life like for you as a child?
What were your parents like? What were their weaknesses, strengths?
Did you have any brothers or sisters? Tell me what each was like.
Did someone close to you die when you were growing up?
Did someone important to you go away?
Do you remember ever being very sick?
Do you remember having an accident?
Do you remember being in a very dangerous situation?
Was there anything that was important to you that was lost or destroyed?
Was church a large part of your life?
Did you enjoy being a boy/girl?

Adolescence

When you think about yourself and your life as a teenager, what is the first thing you can remember about that time?
What other things stand out in your memory about being a teenager?
Who were the important people for you? Tell me about them. Parents, brothers, sisters, friends, teachers, those who you were especially close to, those who you admired, those who you wanted to be like?
Did you attend church and youth groups?
Did you go to school? What was the meaning for you?
Did you work during those years?
Tell me of any hardships you experienced at this time.
Do you remember feeling that there wasn't enough food or necessities of life as a child or adolescent?
Do you remember feeling left alone, abandoned, not having enough love or care as a child or adolescent?
What were the pleasant things about your adolescence?
What was the most unpleasant thing about your adolescence?
All things considered, would you say you were happy or unhappy as a teenager?
Do you remember your first attraction to another person?
How did you feel about sexual activities and your own sexual identity?

Family and home

How did your parents get along?
How did other people in your home get along?
What was the atmosphere in your home?
Were you punished as a child? For what? Who did the punishing? Who was 'boss'?
When you wanted something from your parents, how did you go about getting it?
What kind of person did your parents like the most? The least?
Who were you closest to in your family?
Who in your family were you most like? In what way?

Adulthood

What part did religion play in your life?
Now I'd like to talk to you about your life as an adult, starting when you were in your twenties up to today. Tell me of the most important events that happened in your adulthood.
What was life like for you in your twenties and thirties?
What kind of person were you? What did you enjoy?
Tell me about your work. Did you enjoy your work? Did you earn an adequate living? Did you work hard during those years? Were you appreciated?
Did you form significant relationships with other people?
Did you marry?
  (Yes) What kind of person was your spouse?
  (No) Why not?
Do you think marriages get better or worse over time?
Were you married more than once?
On the whole, would you say you had a happy or unhappy marriage?
Was sexual intimacy important to you?
What were some of the main difficulties you encountered during your adult years?
Did someone close to you die? Go away?
Were you ever sick?
Did you move often? Change jobs?
Did you ever feel alone? Abandoned?
Did you ever feel need?

Summary

On the whole, what kind of life do you think you've had?

If everything were to be the same would you like to live your life over again?

If you were going to live your life over again, what would you change? Leave unchanged?

We've been talking about your life for quite some time now. Let's discuss your overall feelings and ideas about your life. What would you say the main satisfactions of your life have been? *Try for three. Why were they satisfying?*

Everyone has had disappointments. What have been the main disappointments in your life?

What was the hardest thing you had to face in your life? Please describe it.

What was the happiest period of your life? What about it made it the happiest period? Why is your life less happy now?

What was the unhappiest period of your life? Why is your life more happy now?

What was the proudest moment of your life?

If you could stay the same age all your life, what age would you choose? Why?

How do you think you've made out in life? Better or worse than what you hoped for?

Let's talk a little about you as you are now. What are the best things about being the age you are now?

What are the worst things about being the age you are now?

What are the most important things to you in your life today?

What do you hope will happen to you as you grow older?

What do you fear will happen to you, as you grow older?

Have you enjoyed participating in this review of your life?

Bibliography

Adler, A. (1957) *What Life Should Mean to You*, New York: G.P. Puttnam's.

Alexander, C.N. and Langer, E.J. (1990) *Higher Stages of Human Development. Perspectives on Adult Growth*, New York: Oxford University Press.

Allan, G. (1994) 'Traditions and transitions', *Psychoanalytic Review* 81, 1: 79–100.

Alphonso, H. (1990) *The Personal Vocation. Transformation in Depth through the Spiritual Exercises*, Rome: C.I.S.

Aumann, G.M.-E. and Cole, T.R. (1991) 'In whose voice? Composing a lifesong collaboratively', *Journal of Clinical Ethics* 2: 45–9.

Baltes, P.B., Reese, H.W. and Lipsitt, L.P. (1980) 'Life-span developmental psychology', *Annual Review of Psychology* 31: 65–110.

Bazant, J. (1992) 'Personal recollections and music. A review', Psychology Department, University of Leicester.

Bender, M., Bauckham, P. and Norris, A. (1998) *The Therapeutic Purposes of Reminiscence*, London: Sage.

Benson, H. (1996) *Timeless Healing. The Power and Biology of Belief*, London: Simon & Schuster.

Berne, E. (1974) *What Do You Say After You Say Hello? The Psychology Of Human Destiny*, London: Andre Deutsch.

Birren, J.E. (1987) 'The best of all stories. Autobiography gives new meaning to our present lives by helping us understand the past more fully', *Psychology Today*, May, 91–2.

Birren, J.E. and Birren, B.A. (1995) 'Guided autobiography: exploring the self and encouraging development', in J.E. Birren, G. Kenyon, J.-E. Ruth, J.J.F. Schroots and T. Svensson (eds) *Aging and Autobiography: Explorations in Adult Development*, New York: Springer.

Birren, J. and Deutchman, D. (1991) *Guiding Autobiography Groups for Older Adults*, Baltimore, MD: Johns Hopkins University Press.

Blackmore, S. (1999) *The Meme Machine*, Oxford: Oxford University Press.

Bornat, J. (ed.) (1994) *Reminiscence Reviewed. Perspectives, Evaluations, Achievements*, Buckingham: Open University Press.

Boscolo, L. and Bertrando, P. (1993) *The Times of Time. A New Perspective in Systemic Therapy and Consultation*, New York: Norton.

Boylin, W., Gordon, S.K. and Nehrke, M.F. (1976) 'Reminiscing and ego integrity in elderly institutionalized males', *Gerontologist* 16: 118–24.

Bright, R. (1997) *Wholeness in Later Life*, London: Jessica Kingsley.

Brink, T.L. (1979) *Geriatric Psychotherapy*, New York: Human Sciences Press.

Bromley, D.B. (1988) *Human Ageing. An Introduction to Gerontology*, Harmondsworth: Penguin.

—— (1990) *Behavioural Gerontology. Central Issues in the Psychology of Ageing*, Chichester: Wiley.

Butler, R.N. (1963) 'The life review: an interpretation of reminiscence in the aged', *Psychiatry* 26: 65–76.

—— (1975) *Why Survive? Being Old in America*, New York: Harper & Row.

Byng-Hall, J. (1995) *Rewriting Family Scripts. Improvisation and Systems Change*, New York: Guilford Press.

Cameron, P. (1972) 'The generation gap: time orientation', *Gerontologist* 12, 11: 117–19.

Chodorow, N. (1978) *The Reproduction of Mothering. Psychoanalysis and the Sociology of Gender*, Berkeley, CA: University of California Press.

Chubon, S. (1980) 'A novel approach to the process of life review', *Journal of Gerontological Nursing* 10: 543–6.

Clarkson, P. (1999) *Gestalt Counselling in Action*, London: Sage.

Cohen, G. (1996) *Memory in the Real World*, Hove: Psychology Press.

Cohler, B.J. and Jenuwine, M.J. (1995) 'Suicide, life course, and life story', *International Psychogeriatrics* 7, 2: 199–219.

Coleman, P.G. (1974) 'Measuring reminiscence characteristics from conversation as adaptive features of old age', *International Journal of Aging and Human Development* 8: 281–94.

—— (1986) *Ageing and Reminiscence Processes. Social and Clinical Implications*, Chichester: Wiley.

—— (1988) 'Mental health in old age', in B. Gearing, M. Johnson and T. Heller (eds) *Mental Health Problems in Old Age. A Reader*, Chichester: Wiley.

Conway, M.A. (1990) *Autobiographical Memory. An Introduction*, Milton Keynes: Open University Press.

Costa, P.T. and Kastenbaum, R. (1967) 'Some aspects of memories and ambitions in centenarians', *Journal of Genetic Psychology* 110: 3–16.

Crossley, M.L. (2000) *Introducing Narrative Psychology. Self, Trauma and the Construction of Meaning*, Buckingham: Open University Press.

Davies, J.B. (1978) *The Psychology of Music*, London: Hutchinson.

DeSalvo, L. (1999) *Writing as a Way of Healing*, London: Women's Press.

DeVries, B. and Watt, D. (1996) 'A lifetime of events: age and gender variations in the life story', *International Journal of Aging and Human Development* 42, 2: 81–102.

Dien, D.S. (1983) 'Big me and little me. A Chinese perspective on self', *Psychiatry* 46, 3: 281–6.

Dobrof, R. (1984) 'Introduction: a time for reclaiming the past', in M. Kaminsky (ed.) *The Uses of Reminiscence: New Ways of Working with Older Adults*, New York: Haworth Press.

Dreyfus, H.L. and Dreyfus, S.E. (1986) *Mind Over Machine*, New York: Free Press.

Edinberg, M.A. (1985) *Mental Health Practice with the Elderly*, Englewood Cliffs, NJ: Prentice-Hall.

Egan, G.E. (1998) *The Skilled Helper. A Problem-management Approach to Helping*, Pacific Grove, CA: Brooks/Cole.

Elsbree, L. (1982) *The Rituals of Life: Patterns in Narrative*, New York: Kennikat.

Erikson, E.H. (1963) *Childhood and Society*, New York: Norton.

—— (1980) *Identity and the Life Cycle: A Reissue*, New York: Norton.

Eulert, C.H. (1998) *The Magic Chest. Where You Are, Where You've Been, Where You're Going*, New York: Taylor & Francis.

Fallott, R.D. (1980) 'The impact of mood on verbal reminiscing in late adulthood', *International Journal of Aging and Human Development* 10: 385–400.

Firestone, R.W. (1997) *Combating Destructive Thought Processes. Voice Therapy and Separation Theory*, Thousand Oaks, CA: Sage.

Fishman, S. (1992) 'Relationships among an older adult's life review, ego integrity, and death anxiety', *International Psychogeriatrics* 4 (suppl. 2): 267–77.

Ford, D.H. and Lerner, R.M. (1992) *Developmental Systems Theory: An Integrative Approach*, London: Sage.

Frankl, V.E. (1973) *Psychotherapy and Existentialism. Selected Papers on Logotherapy*, Harmondsworth: Penguin.

—— (1985) *Man's Search for Meaning*, New York: Washington Square Press.

Fransella, F. and Dalton, P. (2000) *Personal Construct Counselling In Action*, London: Sage.

Fry, P.S. (1983) 'Structured and unstructured reminiscence training and depression among the elderly', *Clinical Gerontologist* 1: 15–39.

Galassie, F.S. (1991) 'A life-review workshop for gay and lesbian elders', *Journal of Gerontological Social Work* 16, 1–2: 75–86.

Garland, J. (1994) 'O what splendour, it all coheres. Life review therapy with older people', in J. Bornat (ed.) *Reminiscence Reviewed: Perspectives, Evaluations, Achievements*, Buckingham: Open University Press.

Garland, J. and Garland, C. (1995) 'A person, not a problem. Life review in reframing "demented" behaviour', European Reminiscence Symposium: Blackheath.

Garland, J. and Kemp, E. (1996) 'Doing life review', *PSIGE Newsletter* 56: 9–11.

Gatz, M., Pearson, C. and Fuentes, M. (1983) 'Older women and mental health', *Issues in Mental Health Nursing* 5, 1–4: 273–99.

Gearing, B. and Coleman, P. (1995) 'Biographical assessment in community care', in J.E. Birren, G. Kenyon, J.-E. Ruth, J.J.F. Schroots and T. Svensson (eds) *Aging and Biography: Explorations in Adult Development*, New York: Springer.

Gergen, K. (1991) *The Saturated Self: Dilemmas of Identity in Contemporary Life*, New York: Basic Books.

Gersie, A. and King, N. (1990) *Storymaking in Education and Therapy*, London: Jessica Kingsley.

Gilligan, C. (1982) *In a Different Voice: Psychological Theory and Women's Development*, Cambridge, MA: Harvard University Press.

Goldfarb, A.I. and Turner, H. (1953) 'Psychotherapy of aged persons', *American Journal of Psychiatry* 109: 916–21.

Gould, R.L. (1978) *Transformations: Growth and Change in Adult Life*, New York: Simon & Schuster.

—— (1980) 'Transformational tasks in adulthood', in S.I. Greenspan and G.H. Pollock (eds) *The Course of Life: Psychoanalytic Contributions toward Understanding Personality Development, vol. III. Adulthood and the Aging Process*, Washington, DC: National Institute of Mental Health.

Greene, R.R. (1982) 'Life review: a technique for clarifying family roles in adulthood', *Clinical Gerontologist* 1, 2: 59–67.

Guggenbuehl-Craig, A. (1991) *The Old Fool and the Corruption of Myth*, Dallas, TX: Spring Publications.

Haight, B.K. (1992) 'Long-term effects of a structured life review process', *Journal of Gerontology* 47, 5: 312–15.

Haight, B.K. and Dias, J.K. (1992) 'Examining key variables in selected reminiscing modalities', *International Psychogeriatrics* 4 (suppl. 2): 279–90.

Haight, B.K. and Webster, J.D. (eds) (1995) *The Art and Science of Reminiscing: Theory, Research, Methods, and Applications*, Washington, DC: Taylor & Francis.

Haight, B.K., Coleman, P.G. and Lord, K. (1995) 'The linchpins of a successful life review: structure, evaluation, and individuality', in B.K. Haight and J.D. Webster (eds) *The Art and Science of Reminiscing: Theory, Research, Methods, and Applications*, Washington, DC: Taylor & Francis.

Halberg, I. (1990) 'Vocally disruptive behaviour in severely demented patients in relation to institutional care provided', Umea University medical dissertation, Umea, Sweden.

Hargrave, T.D. (1994) 'Using video life reviews with older adults', *Journal of Family Therapy* 16, 3: 259–68.

Hargrave, T.D. and Hanna, S.M. (1997) *The Aging Family. New Visions in Theory, Practice and Reality*, New York: Brunner/Mazel.

Havighurst, R.J. and Glaser, R. (1972) 'An exploratory study of reminiscence', *Journal of Gerontology* 27: 245–53.

Heckhausen, J. and Schulz, R. (1995) 'A life-span theory of control', *Psychological Review* 102, 2: 284–304.

Hillman, J. (1999) *The Force of Character: A Study of the Meaning of Ageing*, New York: Random House.

Hoffman, B. (1988) *No One is to Blame. Freedom from Compulsive Self-defeating Behavior. The Discoveries of the Quadrinity Process*, Oakland, CA: Recycling Books.

Hubback, J. (1996) 'The archetypal senex: an exploration of old age', *Journal of Analytical Psychology* 41, 1: 3–18.

Hunt, L., Marshall, M. and Rowlings, C. (1997) *Past Trauma in Late Life. European Perspectives on Therapeutic Work with Older People*, London: Jessica Kingsley.

Jacobi, J. (1968) *The Psychology of C.G. Jung*, London: Routledge & Kegan Paul.

Jung, C.G. (1939) *The Integration of the Personality*, London: Routledge & Kegan Paul.

—— (1959) *The Structure and Dynamics of the Psyche*, London: Routledge & Kegan Paul.

Karpf, R.J. (1982) 'Individual psychotherapy with the elderly', in A.M. Horton Jr. (ed.) *Mental Health Interventions for the Aging*, New York: Praeger.

Kastenbaum, R. (1987) 'Prevention of age-related problems', in L.L. Carstensen and B.A. Edelstein (eds) *Handbook of Clinical Gerontology*, New York: Pergamon Press.

Kaufman, S.R. (1986) *The Ageless Self: Sources of Meaning in Late Life*, Madison, WI: University of Wisconsin Press.

Kenyon, G. (1995) 'The meaning value of personal storytelling', in J.E. Birren, G. Kenyon, J.-E. Ruth, J.J.F. Schroots and T. Svensson (eds) *Aging and Biography: Explorations in Adult Development*, New York: Springer.

Kiernat, J.-M. (1983) 'Retrospection as a life span concept', *Physical and Occupational Therapy in Geriatrics* 3, 2: 35–48.

Kimmel, D. (1990) *Adulthood and Aging. An Interdisciplinary Developmental View*, New York: Wiley.

Knight, B.G. (1996a) 'Psychodynamic therapy with older adults: lessons from scientific gerontology', in R.T. Woods (ed.) *Handbook of the Clinical Psychology of Ageing*, Chichester: Wiley.

—— (1996b) *Psychotherapy with Older Adults*, Thousand Oaks, CA: Sage.

Kotre, J. (1996) *White Gloves. How We Create Ourselves Through Memory*, New York: Norton.

Labouvie-Vief, G., Chiodo, L.M., Goguen, L.A., Diehl, M. and Orwoll, L. (1995) 'Representations of self across the life span', *Psychology and Aging* 10, 3: 404–15.

Lang, M. and Lang, T. (1996) *Resilience: Stories of a Family Therapist*, Port Melbourne: Mandarin.

Lesser, J., Lazarus, L.W., Frankel, R. and Havasy, S. (1981) 'Reminiscence group therapy with psychotic geriatric inpatients', *Gerontologist* 21: 291–6.

Levinson, D.J., Darrow, D.N., Klein, E.B., Levinson, M.H. and McKee, B. (1978) *The Seasons of a Man's Life*, New York: Knopf.

Lewis, M.I. and Butler, R.N. (1974) 'Life review therapy: putting memories to work in individual and group psychotherapy', *Geriatrics* 29: 165–73.

Lieberman, M.A. and Falk, J.M. (1971) 'The remembered past as a source of data for research on the life cycle', *Human Development* 14: 132–41.

Lieberman, M.A. and Tobin, S.S. (1983) *The Experience of Old Age. Stress, Coping and Survival*, New York: Basic Books.

Lowenthal, M., Thurnher, M. and Chiriboga, B. (1975) *Four Stages of Life*, San Francisco, CA: Jossey-Bass.

Ludwig, A.M. (1997) *How Do We Know Who We Are? A Biography of the Self*, New York: Oxford University Press.

McAdams, D.P. (1997) *The Stories We Live By. Personal Myths and the Making of the Self*, New York: Guilford Press.

McGraw, P.C. (1999) *Life Strategies. Doing What Works, Doing What Matters*, New York: Hyperion.

McLeod, J. (1997) *Narrative and Psychotherapy*, London: Sage.

McMahon, A.W. and Rhudick, P.J. (1964) 'Reminiscing: adaptational significance in the aged', *Archives of General Psychiatry* 10: 203–8.

Magee, J.J. (1988a) *A Professional's Guide to Older Adults' Life Review. Releasing the Peace Within*, Lexington, MA: Lexington Books.

—— (1988b) 'Using poetry as an aid to life review', *Activities, Adaptation and Aging* 12, 1–2: 91–101.

—— (1991a) 'Dream analysis as an aid to older adults' life review', *Journal of Gerontological Social Work* 18, 1–2: 163–73.

—— (1991b) 'Using metaphors in life review groups to empower shame-driven older adults', *Activities, Adaptation and Aging* 16, 2: 19–30.

Mair, M. (1988) 'Psychology as storytelling', *International Journal of Personal Construct Psychotherapy* 1: 125–38.

Maslow, A.H. (1970) *Motivation and Personality*, New York: Harper & Row.

Masson, J.M. (1988) *Against Therapy: Emotional Tyranny and the Myth of Psychological Healing*, New York: Atheneum.

Merriam, S.B. (1993) 'Butler's life review: how universal is it?' *International Journal of Aging and Human Development* 37, 3: 163–75.

Molinari, V. and Reichlin, R.E. (1984–5) 'Life review reminiscence in the elderly: a review of the literature', *International Journal of Aging and Human Development* 20, 2: 81–92.

Moody, H.R. (1984) 'Reminiscence and the recovery of the public world', *Journal of Gerontological Social Work* 7, 1–2: 157–66.

—— (1988) 'Twenty-five years of the life review: where did we come from? where are we going?' *Journal of Gerontological Social Work* 12, 3–4: 7–21.

Mouratoglou, V. (1991) 'Older people and their familiies: a workshop led by Ruth Mohr and Marilyn Frankfurt of the Ackerman Institute for Family Therapy, New York', *Context* 8: 10–13.

Murphy, M.J. (1996) 'The Wizard of Oz as cultural narrative and conceptual model for psychotherapy', *Psychotherapy* 33, 4: 531–8.

Murray, P.D., Lowe, J.D. and Horne, H.L. (1995) 'Assessing filial maturity through the use of the Filial Anxiety Scale', *Journal of Psychology* 129, 5: 519–29.

Nelson, K. (1986) *Event Knowledge: Structure and Function in Development*, Hillsdale, NJ: Erlbaum.

Neugarten, B.L. (1977) 'Adaptation and the life cycle', in N.K. Schlossberg and A.D. Entine (eds) *Counseling Adults*, Monterey, CA: Brooks/Cole.

Neugarten, B., Havighurst, R. and Tobin, S. (1961) 'The measurement of satisfaction', *Journal of Gerontology* 14: 134–43.

Nitis, T. (1989) 'Ego differentiation: Eastern and Western perspectives', *American Journal of Psychoanalysis* 49, 4: 339–46.

O'Connor, J. and Seymour, J. (1993) *Introducing Neuro-Linguistic Programming*, London: Aquarian Press.

Parker, R.G. (1995) 'Reminiscence: a community theory framework', *Gerontologist* 35, 4: 515–25.

Payne, M. (2000) *Narrative Therapy. An Introduction for Counsellors*, London: Sage.

Peck, R.C. (1968) 'Psychological developments in the second half of life', in B.L. Neugarten (ed.) *Middle Age and Aging*, Chicago, IL: University of Chicago Press.

Pennebaker, J.W. (1997) *Opening Up. The Healing Powers of Expressing Emotions*, New York: Guilford Press.

Perls, F. (1969) *In and Out the Garbage Pail*, Lafayette, CA: Real People Press.

Perotta, P. and Meacham, J.A. (1981–2) 'Can a reminiscing intervention alter depression and self-esteem?' *International Journal of Aging and Human Development* 14: 23–30.

Phillips, A. (1999) *Darwin's Worms*, London: Faber & Faber.

Prigerson, H.G., Shear, M.K., Bierhals, A.J., Zonarich, D.L. and Reynolds, C.F. (1996) 'Childhood adversity, attachment and personality styles as predictors of anxiety among elderly caregivers', *Anxiety* 2, 5: 234–41.

Progoff, I. (1975) *At a Journal Workshop. The Basic Text and Guide for Using the Intensive Journal Process*, New York: Dialogue House Library.

Reinoehl, R., Brown, H. and Iroff, L.D. (1990) 'Computer assisted life review', *Computers in Human Services* 6, 1–3: 37–49.

Richter, R.L. (1986) 'Attaining ego integrity through life review', *Journal of Religion and Aging* 2, 3: 1–11.

Ricoeur, P. (1984) *Time and Narrative, vol. 1*, Chicago, IL: University of Chicago Press.

Riegel, K. (1976) 'The dialectics of human development', *American Psychologist* 31: 689–700.

Rogers, C.R. (1967) *On Becoming a Person*, London: Constable.

Roth, A., Fonagy, P. and Parry, G. (1996) 'Psychotherapy research, funding, and evidence-based practice', in A. Roth and P. Fonagy (eds) *What Works For Whom? A Critical Review of Psychotherapy Research*, New York: Guilford Press.

Rowe, D. (1995) *Guide to Life*, London: HarperCollins.

Rubinstein, R.L. (1995) 'The engagement of life history and the life review among the aged: a research case study', *Journal of Aging Studies* 9, 3: 187–203.

Ruth, J.-E. and Kenyon, G. (1995) 'Biography in adult development and aging', in J.E. Birren, G. Kenyon, J.-E. Ruth, J.J.F. Schroots and T. Svensson (eds) *Aging and Biography: Explorations in Adult Development*, New York: Springer.

Rutter, M. and Rutter, M. (1992) *Developing Minds: Challenge and Continuity Across the Lifespan*, Harmondsworth: Penguin.

Rybarczyk, B. (1995) 'Using reminiscence interviews for stress management in the medical setting', in B.K. Haight and J.D. Webster (eds) *The Art and Science of Reminiscing: Theory, Research, Methods, and Applications*, Washington, DC: Taylor & Francis.

Ryff, C.D. (1989) 'Beyond Ponce de Leon and life satisfaction: new directions in quest of successful ageing', *International Journal of Behavioural Development* 12, 1: 35–55.

Ryle, A. (1997) *Cognitive Analytic Therapy and Borderline Personality Disorder. The Model and the Method*, Chichester: Wiley.

Sundell, S.L. (1978) 'Reminiscence in movement therapy with the aged', *Art Psychotherapy* 5: 217–21.

Santor, D.A. and Zuroff, D.C. (1994) Depressive symptoms: effects of negative affectivity and failing to accept the past', *Journal of Personality Assessment* 63, 2: 294–312.

Schlossberg, N.K., Troll, L.E. and Leibowitz, Z. (1977) *Perspectives on Counseling Adults: Issues and Skills*, Monterey, CA: Brooks/Cole.

Schroots, J.J.E. (1995) 'The fractal structure of lives: continuity and discontinuity in autobiography', in J.E. Birren *et al.* (eds) *Aging and Autobiography. Explorations in Adult Development*, New York: Springer.

Schulz, R. and Heckhausen, J. (1996) 'A life span model of successful aging', *American Psychologist* 51, 7: 702–14.

Scogin, F. and McElreath, L. (1994) 'Efficacy of psychosocial treatments for geriatric depression: a quantitative review', *Journal of Consulting and Clinical Psychology* 62: 69–74.

Sheehy, G. (1996) *New Passages. Mapping Your Life Across Time*, London: HarperCollins.

Sherman, E. (1981) *Counseling the Aging. An Integrative Approach*, New York: Free Press.

—— (1991) *Reminiscence and the Self in Old Age*, New York: Springer.
Silver, M.H. (1995) 'Memories and meaning: life review in old age', *Journal of Geriatric Psychiatry* 28, 1: 57–73.
Smail, D. (1996) *How to Survive Without Psychotherapy*, London: Constable.
Spero, M.H. (1981) 'Confronting death and the concept of life review. The Talmudic approach', *Omega: Journal of Death and Dying* 12, 1: 37–43.
Starr, J.M. (1983) 'Toward a social phenomenology of aging: studying the self process in biographical work', *International Journal of Aging and Human Development* 16: 255–70.
Staudinger, U.M., Smith, J. and Baltes, P.B. (1992) 'Wisdom-related knowledge in a life review task: age differences and the role of professional specialization', *Psychology and Aging* 7, 2: 271–81.
Steiner, C. (1990) *Scripts People Live. Transactional Analysis of Life Scripts*, New York: Grove Press.
Stewart, I. (2000) *Transactional Analysis Counselling in Action*, London: Sage.
Sugarman, L. (1986) *Life Span Development. Concepts, Theories and Interventions*, London: Methuen.
—— (1996) 'Narratives of theory and practice: the psychology of life span development', in R. Woolfe and W. Dryden (eds) *Handbook of Counselling Psychology*, London: Sage.
Sumerlin, J.R. and Bundrick, C.V.M. (1996) 'Brief index of self-actualization: a measure of Maslow's model', *Journal of Social Behavior and Personality* 11, 2: 253–71.
Super, D.E. (1980) 'A life-span, life-space approach to career development', *Journal of Vocational Behaviour* 16: 282–98.
Sweeney, T.J. and Myers, J. (1986) 'Early recollections: an Adlerian technique with older people', *Clinical Gerontologist* 4, 4: 3–12.
Tannen, D. (1987) *That's Not What I Meant! How Conversational Style Makes or Breaks Your Relations with Others*, London: J.M. Dent.
Thornton, S. and Brotchie, J. (1987) 'Reminiscence: a critical view of the empirical literature', *British Journal of Clinical Psychology* 26: 93–111.
Twining, C. (1996) 'Psychological counselling with older adults', in R. Woolfe and W. Dryden (eds) *Handbook of Counselling Psychology*, London: Sage.
Van Deurzen, E. (1998) *Paradox and Passion in Psychotherapy. An Existential Approach to Therapy and Counselling*, Chichester: Wiley.
Verwoerdt, E. (1981) *Clinical Geropsychiatry*, Baltimore, MD: Williams & Wilkins.
Viney, L.L. (1993) *Life Stories. Personal Construct Therapy with the Elderly*, Chichester: Wiley.
Wallace, J.B. (1992) 'Reconsidering the life review: the social construction of talk about the past', *Gerontologist* 32, 1: 120–5.
Wasylenki, D.A. (1989) *Psychogeriatrics: A Practical Handbook*, London: Jessica Kingsley.

Waters, E.B. (1990) 'The life review: strategies for working with individuals and groups', *Journal of Mental Health Counseling* 12, 3: 270–8.

Webster, J.D. (1993) 'Construction and validation of the Reminiscence Functions Scale', *Journal of Gerontology* 48, 5: 256–62.

Webster, J.D. and Haight, B.K. (1995) 'Memory lane milestones: progress in reminiscence definition and classification', in B.K. Haight and J.D. Webster (eds) *The Art and Science of Reminiscing: Theory, Research, Methods, and Applications*, Washington, DC: Taylor & Francis.

White, M. and Epson, D. (1990) *Narrative Means to Therapeutic Ends*, New York: Norton.

Whiteside, R.G. (1997) *Therapeutic Stances. The Art of Using and Losing Control*, New York: Brunner/Mazel.

Wong, T.P. (1995) 'The processes of adaptive reminiscence', in B.K. Haight and J.D. Webster (eds) *The Art and Science of Reminiscing: Theory, Research, Methods, and Applications*, Washington, DC: Taylor & Francis.

Wong, T.P. and Watt, L.M. (1991) 'What types of reminiscence are associated with successful aging?' *Psychology and Aging* 6, 2: 272–9.

Woods, R.T., Portnoy, S., Head, D. and Jones, G. (1992) 'Reminiscence and life review with persons with dementia: which way forward?' in G.M.M. Jones and B.M.L. Miesen (eds) *Care-giving in Dementia: Research and Applications*, London: Tavistock/Routledge.

Yalom, I.D. (1989) *Love's Executioner and Other Tales of Psychotherapy*, London: Bloomsbury.

Young, C.A. and Reed, P.G. (1995) 'Elders' perceptions of the role of group psychotherapy in fostering self-transcendence', *Archives of Psychiatric Nursing* 9, 6: 338–47.

Young, J. and Behary, W.T. (1998) 'Schema-focused therapy for personality disorder', in N. Tarrier, A. Wells and G. Haddock (eds) *Treating Complex Cases. The Cognitive Behavioural Therapy Approach*, Chichester: Wiley.

Zieger, B.L. (1976) 'Life review in art therapy with the aged', *American Journal of Art Therapy* 15: 47–50.

Name index

Subject index